CA$H
FLOW
IS KING

CREATING WEALTH THROUGH REAL ESTATE

CA$H FLOW IS KING

CREATING WEALTH THROUGH REAL ESTATE

AARON MARSHALL

MERACK

www.aaronmarshall.com

Published and distributed by Merack Publishing.
Library of Congress Control Number: 2020915978
Marshall, Aaron
Cash Flow Is King

ISBN: Hardcover 978-1-949635-13-3
ISBN: Paperback 978-1-949635-14-0

Cover Concept by Jimi Scherer

Interior layout and design by Yvonne Parks
Printed in the United States of America

DEDICATION

This book is dedicated to my beautiful wife, best friend, and lover, Andrea, and my wonderful children Adam, Abigail, and Alex. I love you all, and you have helped to make me who I am today. Thank you for putting up with this crazy life of mine as I have worked long, hard hours providing for you and doing what I love in REAL ESTATE and business. Andrea, a special 'thank you' to you for putting up with me and being by my side for twenty-three years.

I also dedicate this book to my parents, Garry and Nancy, who taught me to work hard and follow my dreams. Mom, you would often say, "You get out of it what you put into it," and it stuck. Dad, thank you—you showed me how to work hard.

Thank you to my totally awesome TEAM at the office, both current and past. And thank you, Kelly, for working by my side and helping me the past six years—there are many more to come, I'm sure.

To my business partner Nate who has had to deal with me for the last fourteen years, you have been by my side through the good and bad times of business. Through all the businesses we have together, I value the friendship we have the most; it's truly amazing!

CONTENTS

INTRODUCTION

Growing up, I wanted to be like my maternal grandfather, Harold G. Forsyth. You can see his influence on me in the pages of this book—even lending his first name to the mentor character of our story.

In 1948, my Grandpa Harold founded a very successful company, Apex Die and Box Co. It started as a small plant in Denver, Colorado, where the team of two people spent their days manufacturing steel-rule cutting dies for the printing industry. Within two years, they had grown the business to the point where they needed more space, and they expanded their operations into the die-cutting field; by 1954, the company had incorporated and moved to an even larger facility.

Seven years later, the first of my grandfather's business setbacks occurred—in August 1961, a major fire broke out and completely gutted and destroyed the plant. This meant they had to move again. Then, in June 1965, the South Platte River overflowed, flooding many industrial plants including the Apex facility where, once again, the entire plant was destroyed.

"You can't begin to imagine the damage flood waters can do to equipment," my grandpa Harold recounted in an article he was featured in that appeared in *Boxboard Containers* magazine in February 1974. "Silt got into every gear and bearing and crevice on every machine in the plant. When the water receded and air hit the metal on the machines, there was rust everywhere. Everything with moving parts had to be taken apart, cleaned and, sometimes, machined."

I can only imagine at this point, that he had to have at least *thought* of giving up—but he didn't. He kept going, and he persevered. With the help of a bunch of friends and colleagues in the industry, with whom he'd built powerful business relationships over the years, Apex moved one last time to one of its former locations and prepared to get back to business. It took three months to get the flood damage cleaned up, the equipment repaired or replaced, the building refurbished, and new supplies stocked. In October 1965, forty employees returned to the overhauled plant, and—in spite of it all—no employee had lost any time.

Many of Apex's longtime customers stood by them through this difficult period, and in the same way they rebuilt the physical space, they also rebuilt the company and watched as a pattern of growth began to re-emerge. By the time Apex celebrated its twenty-fifth anniversary in 1973, business was going strong and they were once again bursting at the seams and in need of more space. After temporarily moving their storage and some of their specialty operations to another location a block away from the main plant, later that year they were able to lease 9,000 square feet of space across the street from the main plant, which meant they could transfer skids of stock across the street using a forklift truck.

The business was incredibly successful, going on to manufacture 2.5 million hard bingo cards per year (die-cut cards imprinted with bingo numbers on a small letterpress). They expanded their laminating operations, and they managed the cardboard boxes and paper products for Coors Light—a contract my grandpa Harold acquired over a golf game.

In my eyes, he had it made. People flocked to him, admiring him for his accomplishments and all the wealth he had created for himself. From my earliest memories, I knew I wanted a life like Harold's, where it seemed clear to me (even from a very young age) that cash was definitely KING.

At seven years old, I was out there hustling. I knocked on neighbor's doors, asking to mow their lawns. Over and over again I was told I wasn't old enough to be mowing, so, without skipping a beat, I offered to do the job that no one else wanted—I'd weed their flower beds instead. Although I hated every minute of it, it got me out of the house and put some much-desired cash in my pocket.

That work ethic and drive continued on through my teenage years. At one point, when I was seventeen years old, I was working three jobs. It wasn't long before I realized I could outwork anybody—whether it was in the farm fields or in a restaurant. I was determined to be a success, and earning as much cash as possible was the name of the game.

Despite that belief, I reached my twenties and still had no idea what line of work I wanted to pursue. I enrolled in college, mainly because at the time I was dating the woman who is now my wife and I needed her to feel like this guy she was dating had a vision for his life. After five and a half years of grinding through full-time school and nearly full-time employment, I was approaching the end of my bachelor's degree and I was no closer to figuring out what I was meant to be doing. During my last semester of college, I enrolled in a real estate course—and that decision changed everything. I had developed a budding interest in real estate prior to this, but that course secured my career path. It would allow me to own my own business, like my grandfather, and start building my personal wealth. I committed wholeheartedly and decided to go for it.

Very quickly, my business grew to the one million dollar mark. I was successfully closing hundreds of deals a year, and I was doing what I had always imagined could be possible with business ownership. But something just wasn't quite right. I was hustling from the crack of dawn until well past midnight—pouring my heart and soul into my work—and was always focused on selling, selling, selling to keep business flowing. That left little to no life balance and time off meant less money coming in. Vacations were stressful, and time with my family was always interrupted by potential deals. I knew I had to re-evaluate my vision and the plan for my life, and after studying the people I perceived to be truly successful, I realized that I had been operating under a false assumption—cash was in fact NOT king. It was CASH *FLOW*. If I could have cash flow coming in while I ate, slept, worked, and vacationed, now *that's* what

I really wanted in life. Warren Buffet said it best: "If you don't find a way to make money while you sleep, you will work until you die." And now, after working myself to the bone, I could truly understand why this statement was so true.

I made the decision to begin purchasing real estate to be used as rental properties, one door at a time. That would be my cash flow. While I still hustled to close deals in my real estate business, cash started flowing in from those doors I owned. This change in direction changed my life, and is ultimately the reason I wrote this book. I want each of my readers to know there's a better way than the never-ending hustle and the days of working from sun-up to sun-down, from now until retirement. I've had to work hard and grind to get where I am today, but I do believe no matter where you're starting from, you can build a life where cash flow reigns supreme. By reading this book, my hope is you'll gain the inspiration and the confidence to begin building your own success story, while gaining the necessary tools to start out on your cash flow journey.

Aan Mushall

"Never take your eyes off the cash flow because it's the lifeblood of business."
Sir Richard Branson

CHAPTER ONE
A NEW PERSPECTIVE

"You don't have to see the whole staircase,
just take the first step."
Martin Luther King Jr.

How did this happen? It seemed to AJ like one of the greatest travesties he could imagine—that he should be twenty-five years old, sitting in a rolling chair at a makeshift desk, in an office, in a business park, providing technical support for a product he wasn't even sure existed. (At the very least, it definitely wasn't tangible.) The worst part was that he didn't even know how he ended up there.

"Hey there AJ!" his boss Jeremy, the manager of the call center, chirped as a talking head suspended over AJ's shoulder. "Do you think you could have a write-up of the Johnson account on my desk by the end of today? I want us all to have a pow-wow tomorrow about this one to get some synergy going and round out our efforts—use it as a case study for success."

"Oh, um, yes," AJ responded as he pulled up the Johnson file on his computer. "I'll have that for you before I leave."

The Johnson account had been the only account AJ had managed to correctly diagnose and fix via a phone call in the last month. Working at a call center for North Bell involved a lot of frustrated people asking him to send over a technician for a person-to-person conversation instead of troubleshooting with him. AJ was barely able to get his canned greeting out before he would hear an antagonistic request for a "real" person to come to the caller's house. "You're the best," Jeremy responded, as he tapped twice on the long table that served as AJ's "desk" and then meandered over to the next set of callers. "Hey there Brittany!"

AJ watched him go and shook his head. *How did this happen?* Scarcely before he finished the thought, his coworker Pete's head bobbed along the other side of his section of desk, before stopping to address AJ.

"I just want to say 'goodbye' before I get out of here."

"What?" AJ was on his feet and peering deeply into the contents of Pete's arms before he even realized it. Sure enough, Pete cradled a box filled with manila folders, a stapler, a framed diploma, and a few other knick-knacks his own section of the long table had once housed. AJ shifted his eyes to meet Pete's in amazement, but Pete's face wasn't one of someone who had just been fired—Pete was grinning. "You're... leaving?"

"Yeah." Pete's voice lowered and he leaned in, "I mean, this place isn't exactly where I planned on ending up long-term. I can't stand all of this corporate jargon and doing stuff I don't even understand for a boss who doesn't even really care about me as a person." Pete paused and stole a glance at the boss checking in on the headset-fitted callers at the far end of the long, long line of makeshift workspaces. "I don't think he even knows my name— he had to read it off my resignation letter when he thanked me for my time here."

Following Pete's gaze, AJ also watched as their—well, now only his—boss plastered a synthetic smile on his face as he went down the line, tapping on headsets while they were still on employee heads. AJ didn't even know what the boss's superiors looked like or where the office's headquarters were. As if reading AJ's mind, Pete continued speaking.

"Not going to miss that. I want to have control over what I do and actually know who I'm working for. That's why I'm getting out of this rat race and fully committing to the market here in Utah."

"How is it even possible to have that kind of control?" AJ asked, trying to keep the hopelessness and bitterness out of his voice— and uncertainty of his own success. "And I thought California was the place to be?" "The market is hot in Utah—they're calling it 'Silicon Slopes' and everyone is looking to buy."

"Buy? Buy what?"

"Real estate!" Pete walked to the side of AJ's chair and set his box on AJ's desk. "I just sold my house back in California and I'm using that money to buy an investment property here in Utah." Pete was a California native who had moved to Utah for work several years prior, always with the intention of moving back home. AJ was surprised to hear that not only was Pete leaving North Bell, but he was planning to stay in Utah. Pete's bright eyes and excitement were contagious—AJ found a bubbling feeling of nervous anticipation in his stomach despite there being no reason for it to be there. After all, Pete was quitting, not him. But buying property or managing it seemed too simple. There had to be more to it than that.

"I don't know... that sounds..."

"I had that attitude at first, too," Pete interrupted, "but it went away real fast when I started talking through everything with Harold, the guy who mentored me on how to change my mindset and enter the market successfully."

AJ must have still looked skeptical because Pete grabbed his wallet from his back pocket. After fishing through it, he extracted a business card and handed it to AJ who took it in both hands. The front read:

Harold Marsh
Real Estate Investor
(801) 316-1500

On the back of the card was a simple yet powerful tagline:

Cash Flow is King

Pete continued, "I read this amazing book called *Rich Dad, Poor Dad* and had heard about real estate investing. I really wanted to learn more, but I was scared to get into it. No one in my family or anyone I'm close to ever did this investing thing, and I had no idea where to start. When I met Harold, he explained everything so thoroughly, in simple terms and in a way I could understand. He helped me work through my fear, change my mindset, and have the courage to get started."

"I'll let him know to expect a call from you," Pete said firmly.

"I don't know—"

"You don't know *now*," Pete interrupted again, "and you still might not know when you call him, but I can guarantee if you spend tonight and tomorrow thinking about where you are now and where you want to be—not just career-wise but *life*-wise— you'll *know* you need to do something different than *this*."

When Pete finished speaking, he used one of his now-free hands to motion around at the office at-large. AJ followed the hand's trajectory and stopped at each different item: the nearly windowless walls, the ironically-depressing motivational posters stuck to otherwise bare walls near the bathroom doors, the nearly-empty watercooler.

"You may be right," AJ muttered with a sigh. "Thanks for this," he said, gesturing to the card.

"First thing I'd do before you make any move whatsoever is to apply for a line of credit," Pete advised. "Having a steady proof of income helps to get a new line approved, so you'll want to have that in place before you quit your job."

"Woah! I don't think anyone's quitting their job over here just yet, buddy. That's crazy. And besides, wouldn't I need to *keep* my job to have money to get out of any debt I create using the line of credit?" AJ asked, bewildered.

"If you call that number," Pete began, "and listen to everything Harold teaches you, money won't be an issue. And you'll start thinking about debt differently, too."

That night, AJ decided to take Pete's advice and think about what he wanted in a career. He had always been of the mindset that he'd get a job at a good company, keep his head down, work hard, and eventually have enough to retire. That was the path his father had followed. But was that what he really wanted to do? Work until he was old enough to retire—and old enough to not be able to actually *do* anything he really wanted to do?

AJ thought back to his younger days, when he used to take road trips to Wyoming and bring back fireworks to sell for the Fourth of July. That was when he was truly the happiest—driving from Utah to Wyoming, out on the open road, and then selling to friends, and friends of friends, upon his return. "You're going to want these for a real celebration, snakes won't cut it," he'd say proudly as he displayed his wares.

Fireworks were real goods, a tangible product, and learning the best places to pick them up in Evanston was part of the fun. One time he had come across a collection of stands right on the border, and he spent hours talking with the local firework peddlers, gathering information about the different types available. It was one of his favorite parts of the endeavor.

I wish I could do that again, he thought to himself. *Being my own boss, getting to explore new places, not working in an office. That's the dream.*

Before he consciously realized what he was doing, he found himself in front of his open computer with "apply for credit" entered into his browser's search engine. If he were really going to consider Pete's advice to call this mysterious Harold guy, he should probably take preemptive steps. Besides, he needed to grow up and get some credit anyway. What better time than the present?

———————————

The next day, AJ fell in line with the rest of his call center associates as they trudged to the windowless conference room at the far end of the office right after lunch. To say it was completely windowless was unfair—it *did* have windows to meet fire safety regulations, but they faced the tall wall of another office building and provided nothing but a view of gray concrete. The blinds stayed down throughout every meeting, so, for all intents and purposes, it really was a windowless room.

Even though they were all employed as "technical support," AJ and his cohorts had done nothing but answer pointless phone calls for weeks—nearly every call ended with a technician being sent to an irate customer's office.

Like all of the call center's monthly meetings, none of the associates really knew what it was supposed to be about. At the head of the table, Jeremy kept a stack of papers to his right.

Allegedly, one read "Agenda" at the top, but had nothing listed below it. Once, Pete had sworn to AJ that he had spotted the blank sheet during a meeting and AJ had kept an eye out for it ever since. It had become a ridiculous game that was one of the only things that kept AJ awake and paying even an ounce of attention.

"OK, do we have everyone in here?" Jeremy didn't wait for a response before continuing. "We've had a productive month, securing many new clients and maintaining older accounts. We have AJ here to give a synopsis of this month's progress."

Jeremy gestured to AJ—a cue to start speaking. But AJ just stared back at him blankly. No one had informed him he'd be sharing anything at this meeting, let alone progress for the past month. Had they even made progress in the last month?

"Oh, right, I forgot to give you back the case study you filed yesterday," Jeremy exclaimed with a laugh. He slid the stapled packet of papers down the table until they came to rest neatly in front of AJ.

Grabbing the packet from the table, AJ managed to flip to the first page in the process of lifting the packet into his field of vision. Although tempted to use it as a shield against the gaze of his coworkers, he refrained. Instead, he began to read the report in a voice he hoped wasn't robotic, adding as much inflection as he could to what he deemed to be a technical, boring piece of garbage. But as he read, he noticed he was no longer paying attention to the words he was saying—it had become an automatic path between eyes and mouth, completely bypassing his brain.

I have to stop living my life on autopilot. I hate this job. I hate working for someone else. I need to do something I love.

"Um, AJ," Jeremy began hesitantly, "is that… in the report?"

Bewildered, AJ let the packet fall to the table and surveyed the faces sitting around him. A couple of people were stifling laughs while others were nodding in agreement. Jeremy looked concerned. That's when it hit AJ—he had said that out loud.

"Oh. No. I'm sorry," AJ muttered. He picked up the papers to resume reading when he realized he didn't want to. He had never experienced such an aversion to doing something so simple in his life. His eyes met Jeremy's.

Rolling his eyes, Jeremy motioned for the report and AJ wordlessly slid it back to him. As Jeremy took up the task of relating the snippets of conversation AJ had on the only successful troubleshooting phone call the center had had in a long time, AJ's mind wandered to Silicon Slopes and anywhere but North Bell.

"In conclusion, I think this makes a nice script for you all to follow on future customer phone calls. This should, hopefully, cut down on the number of technicians we have to send out."

The sounds of chairs scraping and the flurry of bodies rising pulled AJ from his mental travels back to the windowless conference room. Immediately, he noticed Jeremy's intense stare.

"AJ, would you mind meeting me in my office in five? Thanks."
Even though Jeremy had phrased it as a question, AJ knew
it was a command. Which is why he took that five minutes
to splash water on his face in the restroom and give himself a
pep talk for what he assumed was the inevitable reprimand for
failing to perform.

Rapping lightly on Jeremy's office door, AJ waited for a voice
to invite him inside before entering. The interior of the office
was a smaller version of the conference room, complete with a
singular window facing the wall of another building. *Was it the
same building? Was this building surrounded by other buildings on
all sides?* AJ was one part embarrassed and one part amused that
he didn't actually even know the answer to this question after
working there this long.

"I want to have an honest conversation with you, AJ. Sit
down, please."

Grabbing the only available chair—a metallic folding one with
strategically-placed padding on the seat and the miniscule
backrest—AJ prepared himself to be admonished.

"As you know, we've gone through some changes in the past
year and a half." Jeremy paused to take a sip of the coffee on his
desk. "What do you think about the changes? How do you feel
about the new way we operate?"

"Honestly?" AJ was hesitant to share his true feelings about
the company.

"Yes, honestly. Your comment in the meeting and general disinterest leads me to believe you have feelings about the company and I want to know them. What have you been hearing from other people? What is morale like?"

"Wellllll," AJ elongated the word and let it lead into a rush of sentences. "Frankly, it sucks. You've taken away all of our benefits. Nobody's gotten a raise since the sale. Everything is more strict—we feel like we're chained to our desks and locked to our phones. The truth is, nobody likes it here. We don't even have windows."

Jeremy waved a hand at the window directly behind him, as if to point out that AJ was flat-out lying.

"You've got to be kidding, Jeremy. That's not a *window*. That's a piece of glass between us and a wall."

With a raised eyebrow, Jeremy scribbled a few notes on a yellow legal pad at the edge of his desk. He paused to chew on the pen's cap and briefly glanced at AJ before continuing to write. Finally, he set the pen down and fixed his eyes on AJ's.

"That's all, AJ," he said with feigned nonchalance. "You're free to go."

As he walked out of Jeremy's office and headed to his portion of the long table, an eerie feeling crept into AJ's gut. Unsettled by the conference room meeting and the undefined private meeting with Jeremy, AJ decided to look more deeply into Pete's referral.

It had only been about an hour since AJ left the office in Provo. Now, he sat alone in the driver's seat of his car, parked just outside of Salt Lake City, contemplating his next move—he had to start planning for something beyond the call center and North Bell. Compelled to start making changes now, AJ felt strangely at ease when he dialed the number on the card Pete had given him. Even though he didn't quite know what to expect, he figured it couldn't be worse than the office he had just left.

Nothing like a cityscape to help you take hold of your future, he thought as he waited for the call to connect.

"This is Harold," a voice greeted from the phone AJ held to his ear.

"Uh, hi. I'm AJ—"

"Oh, yes! Pete's friend from his old office job," the voice affirmed. "He told me you'd be calling. I must admit, though, based on what Pete told me, I didn't expect it to be so soon."

"I'm sorry—I didn't mean to bother you."

"Stop right there, young man," the voice replied and then broke off into a hearty chuckle. "I didn't say it was a bother. If anything, it means you're ready for a change—you didn't have to think too long and hard about it. I can tell from the get-go that there *is* something we're going to need to work on before we really get started, however, and that's your confidence. Rather than apologizing and thinking you're bothering me, to be successful in business you're going to need to grab life by the horns and go after it. You're going to need to ask for what you want," Harold began.

"Well, I guess I don't really know what I want," AJ admitted. "I just know I have a weird feeling about my current job, but at the same time I'm nervous to leave it without a sure thing."

"What does 'a sure thing' mean to you?"

"Knowing I have a paycheck coming in and opportunities to grow…" AJ interrupted himself. "I did take Pete's advice and I opened a new line of credit, but I want to make sure I can pay it off and maintain a respectable lifestyle in the process."

"When I was growing up, I was like you," Harold reminisced. "I cared so much about my surroundings and about what people thought of me."

Flustered, AJ scampered to defend himself quickly, "No, not me. I don't care what other people think!"

"But you do," Harold continued. "You're measuring yourself against society's expectations. Is what constitutes a 'respectable lifestyle' your idea or someone else's?"

In that moment, AJ knew the words coming out of his phone's receiver were some of the most pointedly-true sentiments he had ever heard.

Harold proceeded, "*Now,* at this stage of my life, I could honestly care less. These days, I care only about what my family thinks, and most importantly what *I* think. And I've made it a point to teach my kids the same thing."

"My dad was a computer programmer and always pushed me to head in that direction," AJ lamented. "He never really talked to me about *my* goals or what *I* thought."

Good-humored laughter came over the airwaves. AJ felt affronted at first, until Harold explained his amusement.

"I understand where you're coming from there," Harold said while still chuckling. "I grew up around computers—I remember the first time I saw a mouse when my dad's friend brought over an Apple laptop with one. I was convinced my keyboard and joystick were better."

"So, how does your technology background fit into what you do now?" AJ paused to examine Harold's card again. "Real estate and... cash flow?"

"That's a bit of a story."

Suddenly, a thought occurred to AJ and he felt embarrassed for intruding on Harold's evening. He had mentioned a wife and kids—he was probably just about to sit down to dinner with them.

"Oh, man, Mr. Marsh, I didn't mean to take up your family time. I'm sorry I didn't even ask if now was a good time to talk. I'm just excited to hear about other people's... " AJ searched for the right word to convey his displeasure with his job, his pastimes, his future, "... lives."

"It's quite alright, AJ. I wouldn't have taken the call if I didn't have a little time. Instead of going into my story, let me tell you about how my teenage daughter became less concerned about what people thought of her. I think that would benefit you. And prepare you to think about your goals." Harold paused before he repeated himself, "*Your* goals."

"See, my teenage girl was so concerned about what people thought about her that she was afraid of her own shadow. Over the past year, my wife and I have worked with her to change that mindset. Because a mindset shift is where it all starts."

"How'd you do that?" AJ thought it sounded too simple—there must have been more to it.

"She was so fearful of talking to people. We would go out to dinner and she would want us to order her meal for her." Harold shook his head and laughed. "We'd tell her, 'If you want food to eat, you've got to order the meal yourself.' And we gave her language and support to do that. We started with the small things, and were persistent in having her take action and ask for what she wanted herself."

"Like you're telling me I should do. Ah, I get that," AJ commented, pleased with his skills of deduction.

"Exactly," Harold confirmed, "Then, the next thing she was afraid to do was to talk to boys she liked. I said, 'Well, Mike down the street is a boy—what's the difference between talking to him versus a boy that you like? Do you care if a boy comes and talks to you even if you don't think he's cute?' We worked on having the same level of confidence across the board no matter *which* boy she was talking to."

A small part of AJ twinged with recognition—hadn't he been having the same experience with women in his life? Embarrassed that he had so much in common with a teenager, he refocused his attention back onto Harold's words. "My wife worked to change our daughter's mindset about clothing. When my daughter would say, 'What should I wear? Should I wear this or this? I can't wear that because I wore it already this week,' my wife would patiently ask her, 'What did Tiffany wear this week?' When my daughter couldn't answer—because she didn't remember, my wife would say, 'Well, I'm pretty sure your friends won't be able to remember what you wore on Monday, either.' By making that point, my wife was able to have our daughter step back and get out of the mindset that other people's opinions mattered so much."

AJ nodded enthusiastically as Harold spoke. It was so simple—deceptively simple—to realize stepping outside of yourself could provide such clarity. Then he remembered Harold couldn't see him and replied, "Makes sense to me."

"So if you're ready to harness the confidence you'll need to build a great business and the life of your dreams, let's get off the phone and get started. It's dinnertime for me—meet me tomorrow at my workplace? We'll sit down together and talk more."

"Of course," AJ replied quickly, without a moment's hesitation. "I really appreciate this, Harold. Where is your office? And what time shall I meet you?"

"I'll shoot you a text with everything you need to know. For now, just focus on your confidence and being able to ask for what you want in pursuit of your dreams."

The phone call ended and AJ found himself staring over the Salt Lake City horizon; never before had AJ really taken the time to look at the city from a distance. For a metropolis in the middle of two mountain ranges that was technically in the desert, he suddenly realized it had a lot of greenery—it suddenly seemed so inviting.

AJ laughed to himself. *A new perspective.*

ACTION ITEMS:

1. Play detective and explore your own beliefs. Look closely at your life, thoughts and internal barriers— have other people's opinions or preconceived notions made their way into your own?

2. It's much easier to think of all the things we can't do than the things we can. Make a list of statements that start with "I Can't…" and then go through each one, looking for ways to turn these negative statements into something possible. Can you gain a new perspective?

BEST PRACTICE:
Apply for a line of credit while you are employed and earning consistent income. Use this only for expenses related to your cash flow business.

CHAPTER TWO
A MINDSET SHIFT

"You begin to fly when you let go of self-limiting
beliefs and allow your mindand aspirations to rise to
greater heights."
Brian Tracy

As Harold had requested, AJ met with him at his office the
following day, ready to take the first steps on his journey to
becoming his own boss. But "office" wasn't quite the right
word—Harold had texted AJ an address of a coffee shop in
downtown Salt Lake. Harold was at a place in his life and career
where his work was geographically irrelevant, and he had the
freedom to work wherever—and whenever—he liked. The
coffee shop fit his needs perfectly, it was comfortable and he
had come to know the staff. The hum and energy of the place
provided just the right amount of people watching and noise
without it being too much of a distraction. As AJ learned when
he first arrived, Harold drank hot black tea in the morning

and switched to green tea in the afternoon, so he could always rely on his "office" to have an ample supply of what he needed, when he wanted it. And true to form, Harold was now sipping a mug of English Breakfast in between sentences as he spoke.

"Good to see you're here on time. Showing up in life is at least half the battle, and showing up on time is a critical detail that many overlook as an important ingredient for success," Harold began.

"Well, I've always had that going for me," AJ responded. "Ever since I started working, I've always showed up—you can't do work if you're not there."

"That's the best attitude to have, AJ. Even when you don't have someone looking over your shoulder—especially when you don't have someone looking over your shoulder—work needs to get done."

"Yesterday we ended our conversation talking about going after your dreams." Harold paused and made deliberate, fixed eye contact with AJ. "You need to really go after them. And I'm not talking to the proverbial 'you'—I'm telling you, *AJ*, to go after what you want and don't let anybody get in the middle of that.

"Our minds are the most powerful things in the world." Harold tapped his head. "We let our self doubt and all of our insecurities creep in a little too much. Can you think of a time you doubted yourself, AJ?"

Laughter escaped AJ's lips before he could stop it. He recovered quickly and responded, "Every day, honestly."

"What does that self-doubt sound like?"

"Well, I say, 'I want to own a business or be my own boss,' but then I think, 'Oh, man, I can't do that. Not me. I can't do this.'"

"Why not you?" Harold asked.

"I just don't think I'm equipped."

Taking another sip of his tea, Harold seemed to reach the end of the contents of his mug. As such, he upped the bottom of the cup and sat back in contentment, using his napkin to pat his lips dry.

"Well, I tell my kids, you are what you say you are. And it's no different for you or anyone else, AJ," Harold said. "My oldest son has now graduated but I distinctly remember him coming home from his first day of kindergarten and saying, 'Oh, I hate school.'"

"Already? That young?" AJ laughed.

Harold chuckled and continued on, "I knew he was going to have a hard time with that attitude. He did that for the whole first week. At the end of that week, I said, 'Son, if you can make it a whole week, next week, without saying you hate school, I'll give you a dollar.'"

"Did it work?"

"You betcha. Money is a great incentive and motivator for certain people. He went a whole week without saying he hated school. And it helped change his overall attitude—and mindset.

My kid ended up graduating with a 3.89 GPA. He graduated on the Honor Roll, and I one-hundred-percent believe it was because he changed who he thought he was in relation to school. Once he stopped saying he hated school, he was open to a new possibility. And then once he didn't hate school anymore, a new reality replaced the old one."

"So you're saying the first step is to stop saying 'not me'?"

"Exactly. Follow your passion and dreams, but whatever your passion and dreams are, most likely they're going to require some money. So don't say 'not me' about money either."

"I don't think I'd say anything against money," AJ joked.

"I feel the need to mention it, because I've met too many people who want to own a business, and then in the end they feel greedy making a profit, as though somehow being rich is a sin. I'll be right back. Want anything?"

"No, thanks."

Harold rose from the table, took his mug, and approached the café counter. In his absence, AJ pulled out a small memo pad from his messenger bag. In it, he wrote down Harold's advice about shifting his mindset to one of "Why *not* me?" While AJ scribbled, Harold settled back into his seat, now equipped with an iced drink.

"Green tea," he said, motioning to the beverage. "Anyway, if you want a successful business, you need to make a profit. And striving to do so is anything BUT greedy. A profit makes the business thrive and survive. If your business isn't turning a profit, you're actually doing a disservice to yourself and everyone you employ. You end up bringing in all of this business in the beginning, and then you need help so you start to bring on employees, one by one. Your expenses go up because you're paying all of these people, and then you wind up having to let them go because the business isn't profitable."

"How do you avoid falling into that trap?"

"The journey begins with mindset," Harold answered. "And that's going to be your first assignment. See, when I was young, I thought I wanted to retire at forty; then, at the age of thirty-nine, I guess you could say I kind of did that. I sold my real estate business and could have called it quits and retired. But my mindset has always been about growth, and the idea of retirement didn't sit well with me once I stared it down the throat. Instead, I put all my chips on the table, started a new business, and went for it. Your homework is going to be training your mindset and thinking about your long-term profit goals and passions."

"What do you mean 'long-term profit goals?' Can you give me an example?" AJ jotted down his "homework" but still wasn't exactly sure what he was supposed to do.

"Let's see... right now, my own long-term goal is to have my Health Savings Account (HSA) be self-funding," Harold offered. "This means I'm putting money into my HSA every year, having that buy real estate, and creating cash flow within my HSA. Who has had too much money in their HSA that they haven't been able to use it? Nobody! I'm getting older and costs for everything are going to increase. We can never have too much money in either our HSA or in our individual retirement accounts (IRA). Instead of just having money that sits there, I'll have cash flow. Which is what you want."

"Cash flow?"

"Exactly. You've probably heard the phrase 'Cash is King,' right? Well, it isn't. Cash *FLOW* is King—not cash. Without the flow, cash dries up like a well in the desert." A broad smile flashed across Harold's face.

"Let's recap," he said. "Your first mindset shift is to have the confidence and belief that you can do anything you set your mind to. The second is that Cash Flow is King—having your money work *for* you instead of just having it sit in a bank account. Your homework is to itemize your limiting beliefs and write down what your ideal figures are for middle age. Then, we can talk about how to get there."

Eager to please, AJ started mentally making a list before he even crossed the invisible borders of downtown. He narrowed his long-term goals down to three specific things:

Be my own boss.

Generate enough passive income to travel freely at any time.

Always have an emergency fund for unforeseen life events.

Wait, AJ thought, *'be my own boss' needs more of a mindset shift—I need to believe I have power over my life and the ability to make my own income without oversight.* So he revised:

1. Make more than enough money to always be my own boss.

2. Generate enough passive income to travel freely at any time.

3. Always have an emergency fund for unforseen life events.

Pleased with his long-term profit goals, AJ headed south to his Provo apartment.

––––––––––

But that Monday at North Bell, AJ's slow build up to entrepreneurship derailed. Just as he draped his coat over the same rolling chair he sat in daily while chained to his pseudo-desk by a headset and a call quota he had to meet, Jeremy strolled out of his office, hands hidden in his pockets and his face pulled into the facsimile of regret.

"Hey, AJ," Jeremy said swiftly in an octave well above his usual level. "Do you think I could borrow you for a moment? In my office?"

"Uh, sure," AJ said as he pushed in the chair he had not yet had a chance to sit in.

Without acknowledging AJ's response, Jeremy slid into his office, leaving the door ajar to allow AJ to do the same. Once they were both inside, Jeremy sat behind his desk—there was no chair for AJ. As AJ glanced around the room for something to sit on, or even a surface to lean on, Jeremy peered at him through almost defiant eyes.

"I've been thinking about what you said last week," Jeremy said, suddenly shuffling through the few papers on his desk. Finally, after going through the three or four papers three or four times, he turned one over and read, "'Everything is more strict—we feel like we're chained to our desks and locked to our phones. The truth is, nobody likes it here. We don't even have windows.'"

Silence filled the room and AJ wasn't sure how he should be feeling—Jeremy had quoted him accurately and recited everything he had said last week verbatim. And to this moment AJ stood by those words and would say them again if prodded for another opinion on the office and its work culture.

"I spoke with some of the other employees after you left on Friday," Jeremy began. He let those words hang between the two of them for a moment, almost like an accusation. "They didn't seem to quite agree with you."

"Quite? So, they agreed but not in the same words?" AJ tried to keep the frustration out of his voice. It annoyed him that Jeremy called him into his office to quibble over choice of vernacular. Next he'd probably start saying the office windows had great views and that the quality of a view was really in the eye of the beholder.

The papers fell limply from Jeremy's hands back to the surface of his desk and, as if reading AJ's mind, he stood, hands clasped neatly behind his back like an inverted sign of victory, and gazed out the window. At the exterior wall of another building. To keep from audibly laughing, AJ coughed into his elbow.

After another long moment of silence, Jeremy looked over his shoulder slightly perturbed, as if he was surprised to see AJ standing there.

"I looked over your timecard and it would seem you've only been working thirty hours a week instead of your contracted forty."

Blindsided, it took AJ a second to form his thoughts vocally.

"We had a talk, back in January, and you said it was okay if I left a couple hours early on the days I had class."

Truly perplexed as to how Jeremy had been fine with their agreement during the semester but failed to remember it now, a few weeks after AJ had his degree in hand, AJ scrambled to explain as Jeremy fixed him with a quizzical look.

"Remember? I was in my last semester of community college, finishing up my degree in business management."

"Your coworkers seem to agree that the work environment is just fine," Jeremy continued, disregarding AJ's response. "You seem to be the outlier—leaving early, distracted."

A sinking feeling permeated AJ's gut. He knew for a fact Brittany hated instructing callers to switch off and on their computers. Hannah groaned every time her phone line blinked and she had to don her headset. Pete hated it, too, but he had been the smart one and gotten out. The others—Mark, Ryan, Jeff, Rick—called in sick whenever they could manage it without Jeremy taking note. No one tattled on one another. They all seemed to have solidarity in their misery. Or at least it had seemed that way to AJ.

"So, you want me to start staying the full forty hours every week or work extra hours to make up for the hours I didn't work during the spring?"

A peculiar change came over Jeremy's face. His eyelids fluttered and his lips pursed as if he had just heard something deeply troubling. One of his sausage-like fingers tapped on his chin as he contemplated AJ's question.

"No," Jeremy dragged out the word as if he had not completely settled on its usage. "I think it'd be best if your tenure here came to a close."

"What?" AJ certainly had misheard. "Are you firing me?"

"I wouldn't call it that. I'd just say your and North Bell's future directions are misaligned."

"That's a really politically correct way of saying I'm done."

A snide smile crept onto Jeremy's face as he replied, "You can use whatever vocabulary you'd like. But I'd prefer if you collected your things before your former coworkers arrive. You know—to avoid any awkwardness."

Yeah, because this isn't awkward at all.

AJ didn't have much to "collect." He simply grabbed his coat off the back of his chair and did one last sweeping check of his workspace. Now, there was nothing else anywhere in the workspace that betrayed a hint of his once-miserable existence there. Now, all he had to do was walk out the office door and—and what?

As the office door shut gently behind him, AJ felt the first traces of panic. Cold sweat prickled from his pores and his stomach churned. His body, a few steps ahead of his mind, already started to respond to the situation as what it was—a crisis.

He had a lease—rent to pay. Utilities that cost money. Student loans he now needed to make payments toward. Life was expensive and AJ didn't have anything, or anyone, to fall back on for financial assistance.

"I have to find a new job," AJ whispered to himself as the elevator door shut. Immediately, he whipped out his phone and began to search an online job board as the elevator made its way down.

By the time the elevator sounded the soft 'bing' to say it had reached the ground floor, AJ had managed to locate a viable job listing with immediate interviews available. It was a sales position at Rubbermaid, and he submitted his application before he even set foot outside the building.

Relieved, AJ slid into the front seat of his car. Technically, he didn't have anywhere to be until that evening when Harold expected him at their usual spot in Salt Lake City. Speaking of Harold, he was grateful to have his help and this mentorship in place, but he knew he was nowhere close to launching his own real estate enterprise. No, he needed a steady paycheck and stable certainty. Harold's vision was one to strive for, but it wasn't an answer to this present problem.

AJ backed his car out of the parking spot and navigated it down the familiar route to his apartment. Even though it wasn't a self-driving car, AJ didn't feel in control. He was operating as if on autopilot. It felt as though his vehicle was attached to a track that pulled him along toward everything he was in danger of losing. But when he pulled into his parking spot outside of his apartment complex and really thought about it, he wondered if he was really losing all that much.

A vibration from his phone told him he had a message—he plunged his hand into his pocket with a level of desperation that shocked and worried him. The notification turned out to be an email—an email from the sales job.

> Are you available for a phone interview today? We're trying to find someone for the team ASAP and your experience makes you more than qualified. Let me know.
>
> Best,
> Doug

A surge of hope rose sharply in AJ's chest as he tapped out his reply on his phone's screen. Only after hitting "send" did he feel safe to vacate his car, since it had been the good luck charm that had navigated him safely home despite his spinning mind that was just now starting to slow down.

The inside of AJ's apartment was a mixture of minimalist and meagerness. No art, posters, or pictures decorated the walls, partly because AJ found such things frivolous and unnecessary and partly because he was afraid he may accidentally damage the walls and forgo his security deposit. What he did have was a black wire DVD rack that housed his favorite films, and a comfortable couch in front of a modest television set, separated only by a sleek, black coffee table with a single coaster, and a simple desk over in the corner.

An alert from his phone told him to expect a phone call at 11 am Pacific Standard Time, which meant noon in Utah. This gave AJ some time to prepare. Instead of taking the interlude of time until noon as a break, he retrieved his laptop and began to seek out practice interview questions—he wasn't going to blow this.

When his phone rang at 12 pm, AJ nearly fell off of his couch when he grabbed the phone from his coffee table. Before answering, he took a moment to compose himself—stood up straight, rolled his shoulders back, and let out a large breath of air.

"Hello, this is AJ," he said, trying to sound as confident and professional as he could.

"Hi, there, AJ. It's Doug," a friendly voice replied. "Thanks for being available to talk on such short notice."

"No problem—it seems like an interesting position that I'd be a great fit for." AJ played it cool and casual, trying to stop his voice from wavering in desperation.

"Plus," Doug replied, "relocating to Los Angeles is an added perk!"

It didn't seem like AJ's gut agreed. As soon as he heard Doug's words, AJ felt his stomach lurch uncomfortably. California always touted itself as the ideal place to live, but AJ loved Utah and he liked being in the Salt Lake area in particular. But given the current circumstances, he might not have the option to stay.

"So, AJ, tell me a bit about yourself and your last position— it appears you were there for a little while."

"Well, yes," AJ started, "but I'm leaving because the management and I didn't see eye-to-eye."

"Oh?"

"See, they gave us these scripts and quotas we had to meet that didn't actually help anyone or measure the right stuff. They were more concerned with the number of callers we got through rather than results, the number of people we were actually able to help solve their problems ourselves instead of just ordering a tech to go out. And then the supervisors micromanaged us when the lines were slow and were bothered if we got up from our desks too often, even to just use the restroom or grab a glass of water. Honestly, it was kind of terrible."

AJ knew he should stop. With every word, he broke the cardinal rule of interviewing: don't disparage past employers. But he couldn't help it—the wound was too fresh and as much as he needed a replacement job, the thought of entering a workplace with any similarities to the last produced in him a profound feeling of dread.

"So you're looking for an environment where the management takes feedback?" Doug asked.

"Exactly," AJ said in relief. It seemed Doug understood what he was trying to say. "It'd be nice to come up with ideas and not only have them heard, but have them acted upon."

The rest of the interview went well, in AJ's opinion. Both he and Doug seemed to be on the same page when it came to collaboration and innovation. Which is why when Doug wrapped up the phone call as he did, AJ was taken aback.

"Well, AJ, it was nice getting to know you and discussing various roles and approaches with you, but I don't think you'll be a fit for this position."

"Um… really?" AJ was aghast. "I thought the interview was going well and we had similar ideas about how a business should be run?"

Doug chuckled into the receiver. Inexplicably, this incensed AJ.

"You really want to know why I'm not going to hire you?"

"Yes, of course," AJ almost wailed, "I really want to work for you."

"No, AJ, you don't. I know your kind. Based on everything you've said to me, you're an entrepreneur," Doug spoke patiently but decidedly. "The first chance you get, you're going to jump ship and go off to start your own business. So let's skip all of that and save us both some trouble."

Oh my gosh, AJ thought as he ended the call mumbling some typical niceties and setting his phone back on the coffee table in slight shock. *He's exactly right.*

In the late afternoon, AJ directed his car to the little downtown coffee shop for his meeting with Harold. He wasn't sure how to tell Harold everything that had happened that day—so much had transpired and it was only 4 o'clock. But, by the time AJ reached the coffee shop and approached Harold's table, he had managed to mentally draft a version of the day's events that he felt adequately conveyed his dismay and enlightenment.

"Why did you apply for the Rubbermaid job?" Harold asked when AJ finished his retelling of the day.

"I was worried about not having a steady paycheck. I still am."

Nodding knowingly, Harold took a long sip of his iced green tea and let out a satisfied sigh.

"When I first started in real estate," Harold reminisced, "I had a baby and another on the way. We were living at my wife's grandparents' house, where the rent was $500/month—but we had no money and even that was a stretch for us. My wife was stressed out and hounded me to keep applying for steady work. But I'd receive postcard rejections in the mail and I knew there had to be another way. Much like the Rubbermaid sales manager you spoke with today, I had a few interviewers tell me my attitude and vision was more that of an 'entrepreneur' than 'employee.'"

"I think I agree with him," AJ said tentatively. "But I have bills to pay now—I'm not ready to start a business."

"Get a side hustle," Harold advised. "Drive for a ride-sharing app, or do something to make a little consistent money, but don't fall into the trap of finding a full-time job in another role. The farther away you get from your desired field of starting your own business, the more difficult it will become to get back on track."

Flipping to a blank page of his notepad, AJ scurried to get down all of Harold's advice. He felt desperate, but at least he didn't have a family he had to take care of like Harold did when he started.

"I can tell you're stressed out. Don't be," Harold comforted. "This is the push you needed. It's unexpected, but the unexpected is part of being an entrepreneur. And, honestly, it's what makes it so exciting and rewarding. Let me see that," Harold said as he motioned to the paper and pen. AJ passed it over and watched as Harold began writing a list.

"First thing you're going to do is set up a limited liability company, or LLC," Harold directed. "You can print out the forms from the internet. Once you have that paperwork completed and filed tomorrow morning at the county office, we can move on to your vision while we wait for its approval. Your business is now your full-time job, AJ."

It wasn't until AJ had the notepad in his hands that he was able to read the list Harold had neatly penned for him:

1. Articles of Organization form:
   - LLC name and business purpose
   - Registered agent's name and address
   - Type of management (member-managed or manager-managed) Duration of the company may be provided, but is not required (cannot exceed 99 years)
   - Organizer's name, address and dated signature, if not a member or manager

2. Filing fee

"And you won't need to apply for an Employer Identification Number since you only have one employee, yourself. Just use your social security number. And make sure you get a receipt when you submit the paperwork and filing fee."

Folding the paper and putting it into his pocket, AJ made direct eye contact with Harold who looked incredibly pleased. The crow's feet at the corners of his eyes deepened with pleasure and his lips curved into a light smile.

"This is all for the best, AJ. Go home, get a good night's rest, and we'll hit the ground running tomorrow morning after you drop off your paperwork. Bring your long-term profit goals—I haven't forgotten about that piece of homework and I hope you haven't, either."

AJ was stunned by how fast everything was moving.

Obediently, AJ went online and printed out the necessary forms that night. He filled them out, and looked them over a couple of times to make sure they were completed correctly before putting them safely in his briefcase to take with him the next morning. He signed up as a driver with two different ride-sharing apps and then closed his laptop. With a weight off of his shoulders, he then extracted the sheet with his profit goals. This part of his homework had been completed last week—but it felt so long ago now. He re-read what he had written:

1. Make more than enough money to always be my own boss.

2. Generate enough passive income to travel freely at any time.

3. Always have an emergency fund for unforseen life events.

Yeah, AJ concluded, *they're still relevant.* It was a pleasant reminder that his being fired hadn't changed any part of his process—it just sped everything up. He settled into bed, no longer feeling desperate or trapped. In fact, AJ was feeling rather hopeful.

ACTION ITEMS:

1. Make a list of your limiting beliefs and fears and then address each one. Research who and what can help you overcome those beliefs so you can accomplish what you want in life.

2. Make a list of your long-term profit goals. Do they align with your values and life goals, and are they within your control?

BEST PRACTICE:
Understand the "care and feeding" of an LLC. Know the costs associated with forming an entity as well as how often fees and filings are required..

CHAPTER THREE
VISION

The path from dreams to success does exist. May you
have the vision to find it, the courage to get on to it, and
the perseverance to follow it.
Kalpana Chawla

AJ arrived at the county clerk's office the following morning, right as the doors were being unlocked. Forms in hand, he marched through the door a little too vigorously, alarming the clerk who had just removed her key from the lock.

"Oh, I'm sorry," he said while blushing slightly. "I'm kind of excited."

Laughing, the clerk motioned to the counter and replied, "Then come on in. I'll meet you over there and we'll see what we can do for you."

AJ pushed the papers under the glass window and waited until the clerk approached the counter, collected the forms, and began skimming them one by one.

"OK, great, these are all filled out properly," she confirmed. "Now I just need to collect payment for the filing fee and you will be on your way to becoming an LLC."

AJ couldn't help but notice the giddy feeling in his stomach. After submitting his payment he waited as the clerk printed off a receipt for his records. AJ looked expectantly at her. Were they done?

"It should take about ten days to process this paperwork. You'll receive a confirmation in the mail."

From the county office, AJ went directly to downtown Salt Lake. Despite hitting a bit of traffic, AJ managed to make it to the café before noon. Even if he hadn't glimpsed an old analog clock hanging above the café's cash register, he still would have known it was morning based on Harold's steaming mug of black tea—this time it was Earl Grey.

"At the very beginning, when I was brand new to all of this, my goal on my vision board was a house," Harold reminisced as AJ slid a piece of paper across the table to him with his long-term profit goals meticulously spelled out in black ink.

"And insurance and a steady paycheck too," Harold added. "All I wanted were those three things, because I knew if I had those three things, my wife would feel like I was 'employed' even though I worked for myself."

"I don't have a wife."

"Then you only have to worry about yourself," Harold winked. "Back when I first started my own business, my wife and I would go to parties and people would ask, 'What does your husband do?' and my wife would say, 'Oh, he is currently unemployed and is still looking for something. He just graduated from university.' She said it in such a way that it made it seem as if when you just graduated you got some kind of a free pass for a few months. But in my case this had gone on for two years," Harold said with a chuckle. "She told almost everyone I was unemployed and didn't have a job, even though I was working full time trying to get my new business off the ground."

"But you *weren't* unemployed!" AJ exclaimed, feeling angry and vaguely alarmed about Harold's past predicament.

"Indeed I wasn't," Harold agreed. "I was working my butt off trying to make this thing happen. Starting your own business is more like having a *couple* of full-time jobs. But when you're married, the mindset shift you have to make needs to extend to your partner, as well. For my wife to get on board with what I was doing, she needed to see me have those three things I mentioned: a house, insurance, and a steady paycheck. Surprisingly enough, I was able to make all three happen within 45 days of each other. That was back in 2003.

"A couple of weeks later, my wife said to me, 'Harold, I'm really proud of you. I guess you really *are* employed, and you're such a hard worker.'"

"That must've been a good feeling to finally have her approval."

"Au contraire," Harold replied. "That was the *worst* thing she could have said to me. Mentally I had been so fixated on those three things, that for the next six months, I became really unmotivated."

Flabbergasted, AJ couldn't manage to form a response. In the short time AJ had known Harold, the word "unmotivated" would never have been a word that came to mind when describing him. "What happened? Why did you feel that way? And what did you do to overcome your lack of motivation?" *At least now I know he's human*, he thought. *It's nice to know even a guy as successful as Harold has felt that way before—for a period of six months, no less!*

"I just needed to get a new goal," Harold explained. "I needed something new to motivate me. I decided the next thing to go after was having $100,000 in my bank account. And then when I reached *that* goal, I had to make yet another new, long-term goal to shoot for. It's dangerous to fixate on one goal without realizing you'll have to do something after you've reached that benchmark. As humans we always need to be reaching for more to stay hungry and at our peak performance level."

Harold peered inside his mug and then leaned over to look in AJ's.

"I'm going to get more hot water—try to make morning last a little longer," he said merrily. "Think about what's *beyond* the goals you have listed—think about your vision for the future. I'll be right back."

Harold grabbed his mug and meandered over to the counter. Meanwhile, AJ pulled out his pen, spun the paper he had slid in front of Harold around, and began writing a vision for the future. This time, he didn't limit himself to only financials— he wrote it all.

AJ wanted money, to be his own boss, to travel, and to have an emergency fund, but he also wanted a house and a family he could provide for and the ability to let his spouse decide if she wanted to work or not—a decision she could make freely by choice and not one that would be made for her out of financial necessity. A movie buff, AJ also wanted an in-home theater and weekends off so he could enjoy his favorite films with his family.

When Harold returned, he stood a moment behind AJ, reading over his shoulder.

"A fan of movies?" he asked as he took a sip of his tea and sat down.

"Yeah, I really love just being able to immerse myself in a good story. How about you?"

"I honestly never saw the appeal," Harold confessed with a self-effacing shrug. "I could never reconcile it within myself to pay money to go and watch someone else's work for two hours when I could have been working on my own projects," he said with a laugh. "Unless it's a movie about business. Then, I will say, my opinion usually changes."

"Don't you have your own way to relax and kick back? You must, right?"

"Absolutely. I like celebrating my successes—good food is one of the ways I relax and enjoy the fruits of my labor. Literally. It's important to treat yourself when you've worked hard. For you, it may be building this home theater in the long-term. The short-term could be seeing a new movie that's out. Congratulate yourself, spoil yourself a little along the way, celebrate a win, and then hunker back down, get out there, and do it again. These are solid goals to work towards—both your long-term profit goals and your lifestyle goals.

"Back in 2007, I did something similar to what you just did. I wrote down my goals on a piece of paper, and I put it on my car visor. Six different goals. And every time I pulled my visor down, I'd see those six different goals—make $40,000 a month or $480k per year. And I would read every one of those just about every day. I was amazed that I made every single one of those things happen. But—my question is—is it *actually* amazing? Or is it the result of being hyper-focused and always vigilant to ensure my actions were contributing to the accomplishment of those goals? In our subconscious mind, as we're wanting that end result, our mind helps us put the puzzle pieces together to be able to accomplish what we want in life."

"So, day-to-day, if I'm thinking about my goals and planning for them, then I'll subconsciously start to make connections and see patterns?"

"Exactly. Throughout our meetings day-to-day, subconsciously, we're going to continue to see who, how, and what will help us accomplish those goals we have set out for ourselves. Things we may not realize are important now can come into play five, ten, even twenty years down the road.

"A friend of mine did this with pictures of a house," Harold said while rubbing his chin and gazing upwards in thought. "When I was helping him unpack during his move, he pulled out a vision board he had made years before. It was amazing how similar the house that he just moved into was to the house that was on this vision board."

"Do you think he was measuring every house he looked at against that one?"

"I don't think so. He told me he hadn't looked at that board in years—and his wife had packed that box. Our minds just have a way of holding onto something and subconsciously using it as a reference point. It's part of our RAS, or Reticular Activating System."

"OK," AJ interrupted, "you're going to have to fill me in on what a… a… Reticular Activating System is."

Harold laughed. "It's a network of nerves in your brainstem that mediate consciousness."

"Oh… of course! I knew that," AJ said sarcastically, rolling his eyes.

"You can train it," Harold explained, "or kind of program it, rather, to have different parameters."

"I know I worked for North Bell, but programming isn't exactly my strong suit," AJ replied with an apologetic grimace and a shoulder shrug.

"It's not hard," Harold assured. "Let me give you an example. I have a picture of a cabin on my own vision board, and I keep it in my office to spur more conscious thoughts even though my subconscious already has it locked and loaded. Once I put it there and started to focus on it, I started to see cabins everywhere. I had never noticed them before, and now everywhere I turn there's another one. And based on my experience, I fully expect the cabin I eventually own will be eerily similar to the one on the board."

"But what if I start out wanting a home theater—or even to run my own independent theater—but I realize down the line running my own theater isn't really what I'm into? What do I do if I find out along the way that my long-term plan isn't actually what I thought it'd be or what I even want?"

"Don't worry," Harold responded. "I've been in that situation myself. You aren't signing yourself up for anything permanent. All of your goals are malleable and they may change over time. I originally thought I'd franchise and then take my company public. Then, once I learned more about it, the idea of going public seemed terrible—so much scrutiny is involved with the process. Goals change as time goes on. But if you have a vision you're working toward and if you have the motivation and drive to stick with it, you'll do what you have to do to succeed and you'll naturally, continually audit yourself and your goals.

"Let's go back and talk about the homework I gave you—what are some of your current limiting beliefs, your 'Oh, not me' thoughts?"

Harold leaned back as AJ shuffled his notes to his list of self-doubts. He felt his face start to heat up and he felt a prickle of shame re-reading the list. His eyes scanned each entry, but he didn't want to read any of them aloud.

"Well?" Harold probed. "I can't help you overcome your current mindset if we don't discuss what your current mindset actually is."

"OK," AJ said, taking a deep breath.

"I feel like I'm too young to succeed at a high level, and I'm afraid of getting into debt."

"Good. Let's start with debt."

Harold pointed to AJ's notepad and AJ slid it over. After flipping to a blank page, Harold drew a T chart on the page and labeled one side "Good" and the other "Bad." Then, he wrote a title at the top of the page that read in large letters "DEBT."

"It's important that you understand that there are two types of debt: there's *good* debt," Harold said as he pointed to the "good" heading with his pen, "and there's *bad* debt. Credit card debt, for example, is considered bad debt because of the high interest rates."

Pausing, Harold scrawled "credit card balances" under the "bad" heading.

"Credit cards are a valuable tool for you and your business—you just have to understand how to use them correctly—which includes NOT carrying a balance. Period. Pete told me you went into your bank the same day he told you about me and you secured a line of credit while you were still employed. That was a smart move. And even though I've said that credit card debt is bad debt, I still want you to actually *have* credit cards, and I want you to monitor and manage your credit score and continue to increase the limits on your credit cards over time."

Under the "good" heading, Harold wrote "properly managed credit cards" and then continued speaking.

"As I said, you DON'T want to carry a balance, and you always want to be conservative, but there are some useful tips and tricks and instances I'll tell you about once you get your business started. You'll want TEMPORARY access to capital (over a 30-day period at most)—and the use of a credit card or credit line can be an important business strategy if used responsibly. It's *not* for going out and buying yourself a new TV!"

Again, Harold wrote something under the "good" heading.

"A mortgage is another example of good debt—it helps build credit.If you have the perception that debt is always bad, it's going to be very difficult for you to win at these games or get the money to even begin playing."

AJ mulled over this distinction between good and bad debt as Harold added "mortgages" to the "good" list and added the caveat of low interest at the top of that column.

"Got it," AJ said as Harold finished writing and looked up at him again. "It still makes me nervous, but I can make the shift from all debt being bad to the possibility of some debt being 'good.' And using other people's money makes sense to me. In fact, it's kind of a relief. My initial fear about being too young to be successful actually now feels like it was rooted more in me not having enough money at this stage in my life to be successful. Now I get that it doesn't all have to come from me."

"Perfect," Harold replied happily, "then let's move on to another fear on your list and tackle more limiting beliefs. What was another concern you had?"

AJ grimaced and looked down as he answered, "What if my ideas just aren't good?"

"Let me tell you a story," Harold began. "Back in 2005, Ryan Miller came and talked to my buddies and I about how he had an idea for a piece of furniture. He started the business in 1998, but it just didn't take off and he had to file Chapter Eleven bankruptcy."

"This isn't exactly making me feel better," AJ said with a gulp, as a feeling of fear washed over him at the mere mention of the word bankruptcy.

The café began to grow crowded. The midday patrons were filing in to pick up lunch orders or place food orders to go. Harold finished off his second mug of tea before continuing.

"It will, it will. You see, Miller still believed in his product, even after having to file. He doubled down, and decided he just needed to secure more funding to get the word out and strip away all of his debt. Momentum creates more momentum. Sometimes you just gotta find the funds and get to your future. Do you know those GiantNest chairs?"

"Yeah," AJ responded in confusion. "My friend has two. How does that relate?"

"That was Miller's product. Worked out, huh? You need to adopt a growth mindset and just view failure as a new way to innovate. Business is a game—when you die in a video game, do you turn off the console?"

"No, I respawn and go again."

"Exactly. You're going to need to model your business mindset after the one you have while gaming."

AJ left the café with two new pieces of homework, start being meticulously conscious of any limiting thoughts that crossed his mind and put together a vision board.

Reminded of his early youth spent cutting pictures from magazines of items he wanted to own or thought looked cool, AJ was nostalgically excited at the prospect of engaging in a bygone activity of his childhood. He hoped he could perhaps recapture some of the unbridled hope and opportunity that young age provided.

He decided to really channel his inner child in the making of his vision board. He clipped pictures of home theater systems, a nice house in Malibu overlooking the beach, a few cameras he'd like to own, a decked out home office—the photos all graced his vision board in what he thought was a tasteful and artfully balanced tableau. Briefly, he had considered putting a woman's picture on it since he also dreamed of being married someday, but he ultimately refrained. It seemed weird to him, considering he didn't know what his future wife would look like.

ACTION ITEMS:

1. Create a vision board using images and words that resonate with your goals and intentions. Place it in an area where you can look at it often.

2. Look at the debt you currently have and categorize it as "good debt" or "bad debt," using the parameters that Harold discusses with AJ above. Can you see where you might have a low-interest credit option that can be used as "good debt" for your cash flow business?

BEST PRACTICE:
Write down your goals, both business and personal, and keep them visible so you see them regularly. Make sure that they align with your bigger vision so you can stay on track.

CHAPTER FOUR
FOLLOWING YOUR PASSION & FINDING YOUR PURPOSE

Pay attention to the things you are naturally drawn
to. They are often connected to your path, passion
and purpose in life.
Ruben Chavez

Harold was away on vacation for the remainder of the week, so he wasn't able to reconvene with AJ until the following one.

AJ used the time in the interim to hone in on all of the advice Harold had given him thus far—every time he had a limiting thought or a moment of self-doubt, he dispelled it with a positive affirmation of "*Why NOT me?*"

Following Harold's advice for "now" income, AJ had started his side hustle driving for ride-share apps to earn extra cash while he got his business up and running. In this way, he felt better about having fairly steady money coming in and he was able to practice the skills that would later help him with networking. AJ had already found he received better reviews on the ride-share app when he could put his riders immediately at ease with a friendly demeanor and casual conversation focusing on the rider's life. Conversations he had thus far had varied wildly and included cities he and a middle-aged man both wanted to travel to, recent movies a teenager had seen that he had also enjoyed, and the state of the environment with a doctor on her way to work who didn't own a car due to the effects of automobiles on the planet.

The next Monday, before setting off once again to the little downtown café, AJ neatly folded his vision board—made on a small poster board—and slipped it carefully into his messenger bag. He wanted to show Harold he had taken his homework to heart and was fully committed to making his dreams a reality.

At his usual table not far from the counter, Harold was already present when AJ entered the café and ordered. It was morning and a mug of Chai sat, nearly finished, in front of him. AJ sat down with his own mug of hot chocolate and proudly extracted the vision board from his bag.

"Brilliant!" Harold grabbed the board with both hands and held it up to give it a closer look. "Looks like you've included both the personal and professional. Nice."

AJ returned the board to his bag as Harold took a long sip of his tea and let out a satisfied sigh.

"The first few 'assignments' were pretty light so I could judge your commitment to changing your current life. Starting with dreams and the belief that they are attainable was a necessary first step," Harold said as he shook his head. "You'd be surprised at how many people can't make it past that one. They look at everything they want and yet they can't bring themselves to really believe that they deserve it or can achieve it. I can tell by the care you took with the creation of that vision board that not only do you believe it, you're willing to put in the time and effort on the details.

"I think you're ready. Let's start building your business."

AJ was admittedly excited at this thought, but fear and apprehension seemed to be the dominant feelings in that moment. He felt as though he didn't have the first clue about business, and even though he felt his confidence growing and his mindset was set on "Why NOT me?", it didn't remove the nagging reality that he just didn't have any technical business skills, knowledge, or know-how.

Sensing hesitation from his protégé, Harold paused a moment before continuing while he studied AJ's face, in search of what was causing his reluctance.

"You seem unsure," Harold said. "Are you second-guessing that you want to be in business for yourself?"

"NO! Not at all. And you've helped me understand the mindset piece, too, so it's not even really about confidence. It's just that… well… I'm realizing that I don't really know anything at all about business itself. I went to community college and took a few business courses, but I only have an associate's degree. I'm committed to learning, but shouldn't I at least have *some* business skills behind me before just launching into starting my own?"

"Degrees are overrated in entrepreneurial businesses. Everyone always says, 'Have an idea, get motivated, do something, then profit!'" Harold laughed. "That's all well and good, but it doesn't provide much in the way of any practical steps for the 'do something' part. The first step in building a business is being able to clearly articulate your vision and ideas. Then you're able to get behind it with all of your passion and drive. But it all begins with a clearly-formed, specific idea. I've been using real estate as your framework because it's what I know best."

Upon hearing this, a frown formed on AJ's face. Nebulous fragments floated in his mind, but pinning down a concrete idea for a business proved difficult, even after thinking about it almost nonstop for the past week. After taking a class specifically on marketing, AJ thought it could be a possible fit, promoting products, because it was essentially a form of sales. The problem was the product.

"I like sales. I was originally hired at the company I just left as a sales representative, to get new accounts. But then it just turned into maintenance and monitoring, which didn't really interest me."

"Any other sales experience?"

"Well," AJ shifted and rubbed the back of his neck. "I guess it wasn't exactly legal, but I used to drive to Wyoming and bring back fireworks in the summer and then sell them by word of mouth at marked up prices…"

Much to AJ's surprise, Harold didn't admonish him or even raise an eyebrow. In fact, Harold cracked up and slapped his thigh, interrupting AJ's story.

"You and I have something in common, kid," Harold roared, alarming a nearby couple who had just sat down at a table. "I started my own illicit fireworks stand in Utah back in the day. Of course, we're at the point in our lives where a legitimized product is necessary, but, boy, fireworks are fun—and they practically sell themselves! Grassroots marketing is ideal and effective in that situation."

This made AJ laugh. He made a mental note to add "grassroots marketing" to the skills section of his resume.

"Yes, those definitely were fun days," AJ replied. "And since then, I've never really had any good ideas for another business or something else I could sell. No specific product comes to mind that I feel particularly passionate about—I don't have a 'GiantNest' idea."

"In the absence of an immediate idea for a product or service, let's focus on a new concept—let's work on having you self-identify as an *investor* first and foremost. In business, no matter what your core offering, if you are viewing your business through the investor lens, your chances for success are increased exponentially. So, tell me AJ—what do you think the definition of an investor is?"

"Well," AJ started, "I guess it's a person who takes money and turns it into more money."

"Yes," Harold said. "It's all about the expectation of a future financial return. And can you see how if you go into business purely looking at it with the expectation of future financial return you might make different—and stronger—business decisions than you would if you were basing your decision-making on emotions and passion?"

"Yes!" AJ exclaimed with excitement. "So… are you telling me, Harold, that it's not actually a bad thing if I don't know exactly what I want to do from a passion or purpose standpoint yet?"

"That's exactly what I'm saying, AJ." Harold smiled as he watched AJ's face brighten.

"What a relief!" AJ continued, his voice coming alive with every word. "I know I want to create money and freedom to do the things I've mapped out on my vision board, but I was really struggling with the notion that I needed to be doing something I love in the process. Everyone always talks about 'finding your passion and living your purpose,' and I think part of me was feeling bad that I don't know what that is for me yet."

"For the lucky few who graduate with a clear idea of exactly what they want to do and who they want to be when they grow up, I say congratulations," Harold said dryly. "But for the rest of us, it's a process. And it takes time." Harold looked at AJ directly now. "If you want to know your purpose in life, AJ, it's actually very simple—it's to become the best version of yourself you can be. Full stop. You've been given a set of talents and gifts and desires, and along the way you'll pair those with developed skills and new things you'll learn, and your purpose is to use them all in the pursuit of continuing to become the best 'YOU' you can be to serve the world while realizing your full potential." Harold paused to let the magnitude of his words sink in and to let AJ absorb the importance of this moment before he continued.

"There's an important concept called 'Precession' that I want you to understand," Harold said, looking serious. "It's a term that was coined by the late, great inventor, mathematician, philosopher, scientist, futurist, teacher, and author of more than thirty-five books, Dr. Buckminster 'Bucky' Fuller. He believed that our fulfillment, prosperity and legacy lies in doing work that is aligned with our own truths and for the highest good of all.

"He defines the Law of Precession as 'the effect of bodies in motion on other bodies in motion,' and it states that 'for every action we take, there will be a side effect arising at ninety degrees to the line of our action.'"

"Not equal and opposite?" AJ quipped, remembering Newton's Third Law of Motion from high school.

"Not quite," Harold chuckled back. "But it is a little complicated—let's break it down using a real-life example.

"Bucky loved using the metaphor of the honey bee to explain this concept more concretely. We know that bees are critical to our ecosystem, and their extinction would soon be followed by mankind's; their purpose on the planet is cross-pollination and sustaining life on earth. But as Bucky pointed out—do you think they went about their daily activities acutely aware of this purpose, feeling driven to get out there and save the world for all of us? Of course not. They were merely drawn towards honey. And as they moved from flower to flower, their bodies 'accidentally' gathered pollen which ultimately resulted in cross-pollination and fertilization when they landed on the next one and the next, etc.

"As a precessional effect of following their natural inner impulse, they unknowingly fulfilled their true purpose. It works the same way for us—our purpose resides at a ninety degree angle to our action. This means that if you follow and consistently act on the signals—when it feels right and it keeps coming back no matter how you try to push it away— the precessional effects will follow and your true purpose will show itself to you."

Harold paused to make sure AJ was still following along and grasping the gravity of his words. Noticing Harold's scrutiny,

AJ nodded attentively, prompting him to continue with his explanation.

"It can feel counter-intuitive. We often feel as though we need to have clarity to move forward, but as Bucky explained, it's actually through *taking action* that clarity and confidence is gained.

"And now I bet you can see why we started with mindset, right?" Harold smiled with satisfaction, watching it come full-circle for AJ.

"Ahhhh, yessss," AJ confirmed with deep understanding. "Because taking action without clarity is scary. Venturing into unknown territory is uncomfortable, and it will test your confidence and you'll need to be in control of all of those inevitable runaway thoughts when they pop up.

"I get it!" AJ practically shouted, feeling like he was tracking with his mentor every step of the way. "I need to take action, and through seeing how I feel about each step as I take it along the way, I'll be able to course correct and know which things are closer to what I ultimately desire, and which things are further away from that feeling. Right?" AJ's voice cracked just slightly at the end as he looked to Harold for confirmation.

"Right." Harold smiled proudly.

"So if I were to approach my new business through the lens of an investor, taking action and checking in as I go, I guess my challenge is kind of a practical one. I'm not sure I actually know what the first action step is, what I should invest in, or what business I should start." A look of sad confusion returned to AJ's face.

"We can tackle that tomorrow afternoon," said Harold. "But for the rest of today I want you to think about precession, passion, and purpose. Go back and review your vision board—and just like the bees are drawn to honey, pay attention to what *you're* drawn to. And get some sleep—tomorrow's gonna be a big day."

AJ could hardly wait. He could feel his future calling.

ACTION ITEMS:

1. Make a list of fifty things you love, in no particular order. Include things that energize you or interest you.

2. Make a list of the things you feel are your inherent strengths.

3. Compare the two lists to look for patterns or connections that may help you to identify your passions and areas of expertise.

BEST PRACTICE:
Stop looking for your purpose, and focus instead on becoming the best version of yourself you can be, given your natural strengths and weaknesses. In time, your purpose will reveal itself.

CHAPTER FIVE
CASH FLOW IS KING

Either make your money work for you or you will always have to work for your money.
Marshall Sylver

The following morning, AJ planned to clock a few hours driving before meeting Harold at the café. He started in Provo, figuring people in need of a ride would be headed into Salt Lake City for the day. Who better to provide it than AJ? After all, he may as well get paid to drive the distance he would have to travel anyway to meet Harold in the early afternoon.

Sure enough, as soon as he signed into his account, someone nearby requested a ride to Salt Lake City. It was the first serendipitous event of the day, and AJ hoped it wouldn't be the last.

After putting in a few solid hours, AJ signed off from the app, parked his car, and strolled into the café which had quickly become a mainstay in his life.

"Hello again," beamed the woman at the register. AJ recognized her—she had been the one to serve him on his previous visits. "The usual hot chocolate?"

"Yeah! Thanks for remembering."

"No problem," she replied. "I have to admit; we don't get a ton of hot chocolate addicts. That's usually coffee's territory. You've been in here a lot lately during nearly all of my shifts."

As he took his steaming mug, AJ smiled and noticed an extra bounce in his step as he joined Harold at their table.

"OK, I'm eager to jump right in," said AJ. "Before I left yesterday, you said you'd help me with my question about what first action step I should take—or what I should invest in, or what business I should start…" AJ, overwhelmed, trailed off for a moment before trying hurriedly to explain once again. "I did focus on precession, passion, and purpose overnight like you asked, but I just couldn't stop thinking about what my next steps are—*specific* steps."

"Well," Harold patiently began, "before you know what to invest in, you really need to have a solid understanding of how cash flow really works. Remember, it's not CASH that's king, AJ… cash *FLOW* is king. And if you remember nothing else from our time together, I want you to remember that one key idea. And I want you to really focus on it."

Harold reached into his briefcase and pulled out a blank sheet of paper and a black felt marker.

"As Robert Kiyosaki describes in his book, *The Cashflow Quadrant*, there's a simple table diagram that explains how it works."

Taking the marker, he proceeded to scrawl across the page, dividing it into four quadrants. He drew an E in the top left quadrant, an S in the bottom left, a B in the top right quadrant, and an I in the bottom right.

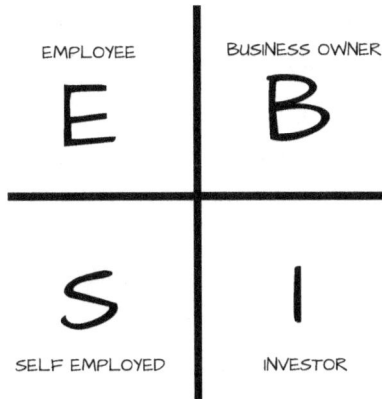

EMPLOYEE	BUSINESS OWNER
E	B
S	I
SELF EMPLOYED	INVESTOR

"E stands for <u>E</u>mployee—otherwise known as having a job; S is for <u>S</u>elf-Employed—people who are self-employed, small business owners who work in their owned-businesses such as doctors, lawyers, et cetera; <u>B</u> stands for Business Owner— and by this he means "big businesses" with many employees, that are selling predefined products and services; <u>I</u> is for Investor—people who commit capital with the expectation of financial return.

"On the left side of the table is active income—the E and the S quadrants—where you're trading time for money," Harold explained. "That means, if you're not showing up every day, you're not earning money. The only way to make more money on this side of the quadrant is to work more hours or find a new company that pays better than the last." The disapproving look on his face told AJ exactly what he thought of life on the left side.

"And although in the S quadrant you *do* own a small business, in reality, that business owns you. The advantages you do have are slightly more financial and personal freedom than an employee does, but the truth is—you're still trading time for money. Think of a therapist, for example. He or she may be self-employed, but if they don't show up for work they're still not getting paid. It's building a *practice* versus a *business* by Kiyosaki's definition."

"Now," Harold's eyes twinkled as he pointed to the other side, "on the right is passive income—the B and the I quadrants—and *this* is where the real magic happens. This is where you're literally making money while you sleep. The big business in the B quadrant implies you have people employed in your business and a system that allows for those other people to work for you, selling a product or a service. You aren't trading time for money, and you don't have to be working for the business in order for it to be generating revenue and profit.

"And the mac daddy of 'em all—the I quadrant—is where true passive income resides," Harold beamed. "Kiyosaki states that there are four main types of investments or asset classes that make people rich," Harold shared. "They are: 1) a Business (with a big B, like we just talked about), 2) Real Estate, 3) Paper (stocks, bonds, mutual funds and savings), and 4) Commodities (gold, silver, oil, etc.). It can also be things you build once that have a long (five to ten years or more) payout timespan—like trademarks, copyrights, and royalties. The genius in this quadrant is that investments like real estate, stocks, and bonds generate the holy grail: annual cash flow.

"The goal is simple," he said as he took the marker and drew a series of arrows onto the quadrants, "to progress through the arrows as quickly as you can, and get yourself onto the right side of the table."

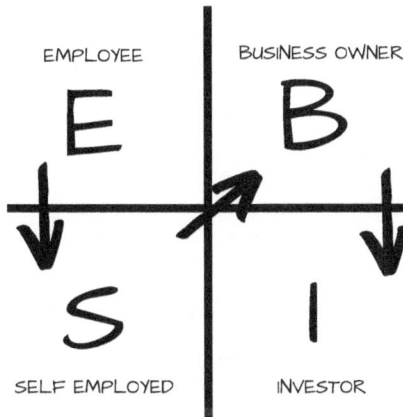

"Wow," AJ remarked, in awe. "Why don't they teach this stuff to us in school?"

What a ripoff, he thought to himself as the magnitude of what he had just learned sunk in. *Everyone I know is doing it all wrong—myself included—and we're actually being taught to do it wrong. We've all been told to go to college, get a good job, and save our money for retirement.*

"I feel like I just got inducted into a secret club," AJ said with a smile. "In the last ten minutes I've literally received the best business education ever—which includes the stuff I paid thousands of dollars for at college," he said with sincerity as he looked Harold straight in the eye. "Thank you."

"Well, kid—knowledge *is* power," Harold said, his tone growing serious again. "But only if you *do* something with it." He paused for emphasis. "So… only one question remains: what are you gonna do with it?" he asked. "That's your homework—decide which of the four asset classes you're going to focus on first: a business, real estate, paper, or commodities. Assuming you've made your choice by then, I'll see you here again tomorrow morning."

When the two resumed their meeting the next morning, AJ felt confident in his choice. He had spent the rest of the previous day weighing his options and deliberating. He even drove out to the same spot with a view of Salt Lake City, where he had first called Harold and embarked on this exciting and unexpected venture.

"I've decided on real estate investing," AJ said enthusiastically as he sat down across from Harold. "I know that's your area of expertise, which may have swayed my decision a little bit." AJ paused to shrug and smile sheepishly. "After spending the rest of the day yesterday researching the four main options, it really felt like a no-brainer to me. It was definitely the option I was most drawn to, the one I feel most passionate about, and the one I think can help me realize the dreams I've put on my vision board."

"Good choice," Harold said.

AJ felt proud of completing his due diligence and coming to a conclusion that he could feel confident about on his own. Harold's crinkled crow's feet and genial smile showed he felt the same.

"I will say, kid, real estate investing has been a great career path for me. For the first four years of building my property management franchise business, I wasn't getting a paycheck. I had gone from earning $400,000-$600,000 per year down to about $125,000, which is a huge difference. I sold five of my properties and made $65,000 to $100,000 a pop on each one, so that was $400-450,000 right there that I was able to put into my business and bring home. It ended up costing me $1.5 million to get my business to break even, versus the $400k I thought it would take, so I had to get creative. I had to look around and see what I could pull together to make things work. I refinanced four of my properties to pull more money out, and I continued to do that every six to nine months as I needed to, in order to make it all happen. And then years ago, when I was going through some really hairy medical stuff, my property investments gave me some truly amazing financial options to help me navigate that time. I was able to sell a few properties to pay for my significant medical bills, and the passive income from my buy-and-hold rental properties gave me the peace of mind that my monthly living expenses were taken care of, so I could take some time off to focus on my health and my family. Very few careers allow a person to do that, AJ. You can think of real estate investing as a business, as an investment, and—to some degree—as an insurance policy."

"Wow, Harold. That's amazing! I'm even more excited now. Looking back, is there anything you wish you'd have done differently in your career that would be valuable for me to learn from your experience?"

Harold smiled, looking off into the distance wistfully as he thought about it. "I think most people would say this, but it's true: I'd spend more time with my family and my wife—going on more trips, etc. I've tried to do a lot of that, but over time you realize it's really the most important thing.

"From a real estate perspective, I'd have bought more properties. Like three to four times the amount. When I was buying two or three at a time and got up to about fifteen properties, I had friends who started around the same time who were getting up to the fifty to sixty-five mark. I had so many opportunities coming to me, and I was nitpicky and would walk away over two to five grand. Now I look back and wonder why I did that. As Robert Kiyosaki says, 'You make money when you buy.' If it works out today, why not?

"And then there's always that 'one that got away.' Whether it's a relationship or a rental property, I feel like everybody's got one. Mine was a trailer park," Harold said with a hearty chuckle.

"I could have bought it for about $1.1 million, but I was like, 'Oh no, I can't do that. I don't have any money.' And I passed on it. Today, that trailer park is worth at least $3 million dollars. Not only is it a prime location, but I'd have bought it at the bottom of the market. It was a fast cash sale, because the owner had a drug abuse problem and was having a hard time collecting rents. When I see the way I was able to pull my resources together over the years to keep my business afloat, I now see I could have done that then, too. But I told myself I couldn't afford it and I didn't have the money. Now do you see why I've spent so much time talking to you about mindset, AJ? In that one deal alone, I lost *three million bucks* because my mindset held me back."

"Ouch," AJ said, wincing sympathetically.

"Well enough about me. Let's dig in. The first step for *you* is to figure out how many 'doors' you need and/or want in order to hit your goals," Harold said as he took a sip of his steaming mug of morning chai. "You're going to hear a bunch of lingo once you get deeper into real estate investing, so let's start building your vocabulary now. 'Doors' is a common method of referring to the number of units—or lockable main entrance doors—a property has. For example, a duplex would have two, and an apartment would have as many as it has actual apartments. And it's often a measure for how costs are recorded, as in 'the annual maintenance expenses for my apartment projects generally run in the range of $150 per door.' Does that make sense?"

"Totally!" AJ exclaimed as he feverishly tried to keep up with Harold's pace while scribbling notes in the new real estate investing notebook he had purchased the day before—a gesture he had made to solidify his commitment by taking action.

"Great. Then let's move on." Harold took another sip of his dwindling cup of tea. "Last night, I started thinking about our conversation from the other day—when you raised your concern about not having the necessary business skills you need for success. I knew you'd eventually get around to asking me about that again, so I took the opportunity to really think about what the key factors are." Harold slid a neatly-typed list across the table to AJ. "And I've distilled it down to a list of ten steps."

The typed list read:

HAROLD'S 10 KEYS TO BUSINESS SUCCESS

1. Know Your "Why"
2. Commit
3. Do Your Homework
4. Talk to People About Your Idea
5. Take Action
6. Don't Give Up
7. Have a Support System
8. Navigate the Naysayers
9. Keep Your Eye on the Prize
10. Be Patient

When AJ had successfully read to the bottom of the list, he looked inquisitively at Harold, tacitly inviting him to expand into a discussion of each one.

#1 Know Your "Why"

"I like to start with the end in mind. 'Where is it you want to be? What is it you want to do?' Which is why the vision board is important," Harold added. "So I start with that, and then I reverse engineer it. Simon Sinek wrote a book called *Start With Why*, and in it he teaches that we need to start with our WHY and then let it be realized through the HOWs and WHATs. It's brilliant advice, really. If I want to have at least a hundred doors that I personally own, what do I need to do to get to that number? What's the end goal? If I want a hundred properties to be my retirement income by the time I'm ready to retire, what do I need to do today to help me get to that point? Do I know about the process of investing? Have I purchased my first investment property?"

"At this point, that all seems so far away," AJ muttered dejectedly.

"But the point is to start accruing the necessary knowledge now," Harold explained. "If you don't know any of those things, then how will you learn them by the time you plan to retire? Start small—say, twenty-five doors. Ask yourself, 'What do I need to do *today* to get to door number one?' Go to investment seminars, surround yourself with like-minded people and research properties.

"Or maybe the end goal is a dollar amount—if so, what is that amount? And how many doors will get you there?"

A worried look must have crossed AJ's face, as before he continued, Harold stopped to peer at him—making sure he was ready and relatively prepared… at least emotionally.

"And it's good to have short-term goals along the way to the big ones," Harold advised. "They could be as small as taking a vacation or as big as starting a family. You already have some of those on your vision board. Those motivating factors along the way will tide you over while you work toward your end game.

"Money can be a motivating factor, but money can only go so far. I've noticed in my own life as well as my business partner's, that if we're in a grind where we're working hard with no tangible payoff, we start to get burned out. It's amazing what happens psychologically and what an impact it has. I've told him, 'Hey, you seem worn out. Go and book a vacation.'"

"And does he listen?" AJ paused his writing, asking the question in earnest. Harold seemed to appreciate AJ's concern.

"Sometimes. But one time he said, 'I can't go on a vacation today—or even next month.'"

Harold swirled the remnants of his chai and stared into the mug with a furrowed brow. He took a sip and looked up before continuing.

"But I told him to book it anyway, even if it was further out. This was in March of that year—and he booked a trip for the coming September. The effect was amazing," Harold recalled, as if he could see the results in present time. "The very next week, his attitude completely changed—he had his motivation back. Having an experience to look forward to did the job. Just knowing that he was going to have time with his spouse, away from the office in the upcoming months, was enough to keep him driving forward. Same goes for you, AJ—remember to make short-term incentives for yourself and make sure they align with long-term goals. Don't buy a boat if you never plan on using the boat, if you know what I mean," Harold added with a wink.

"In my own life," Harold continued, "a short-term incentive is the ability to take four-day weekends with my wife once per quarter. Together, we'll drop into a new city and explore it. For example, we've done Seattle, Denver, New Orleans, San Francisco, and San Diego. And we have a lot of different cities we'd still like to get to—just fly in on a Thursday night with nothing planned and do as much as we can by the time we leave Sunday evening. Spending time with my wife and traveling, away from the office, is enough to recharge me and keeps me working toward the long-term goals."

#2 Commitment

"When my wife really wants something but she doesn't quite know how to put it together logistically, she'll come to me and say, 'Harold, can you do this? Can you just do your magic?' And I laugh because I know what she means."

"What does she mean?" AJ interjected. "What kind of magic is she talking about?"

"She knows if I want something and I'm passionate about it, I'll do whatever it takes to make it happen. It's definitely a mode I have to get in to, but if I set my mind to something, it happens. And for me to set my mind to something, I have to have the motivation from the first step. In this instance, my motivation is a happy wife. And I do what I can to achieve that."

Almost subconsciously, AJ found himself glancing toward the cash register before he caught himself. *Will I ever have that incentive?* Harold seemed to have read his thoughts.

"It takes hard work and sticking it out—even when there isn't 'magic' right away. Without that, I don't believe I'd be where I am today. It's just like any relationship—you make a commitment and work hard to keep the passion alive and it'll return to you tenfold.

"Obstacles aren't an issue when it comes to achieving something. Where there's a will, there's a way."

#3 Do Your Homework

"But will is only one aspect," Harold clarified. "And then you need knowledge. Educating yourself is imperative—it's learning about real estate wholeheartedly, knowing the trends, knowing the valuation process, knowing how to rehabilitate a place—if that's what you're going to do."

"Is that why you keep giving me homework assignments?" AJ was catching on.

"Exactly. Remember—education is not the same as experience because you aren't actually diving in and *doing it* at this point. This is acquiring the theory before you put anything into practice.

"People have come with me to shadow my rehabilitation process—and I've shadowed other people, as well, while I was learning. I asked them, 'You're rehabbing this—can I come by every week and see the progress that you've done in that time?' Doing this allows you to chat with them or their contractors for a couple minutes and get a feel for different types of projects and workflows. 'Hey, why did that renovation happen now? Why didn't you do an alternate fix instead? You tore down this—why not that?'"

"Ask questions to get a feel for what is being done, what's not being done, and why. I did my first rehab knowing nothing, just pretending in my mind that I was creating a place that my wife and I would want to move into. This served as a rough guide for my decision making. Well—let me tell you, that is NOT how you rehab a place! That lesson cost me ten grand to learn, fixing all of the mistakes I made because I didn't know any better. There was a big gap between what I *thought* was supposed to be done and what really needed to be done. And that gap could only be filled with knowledge."

"How do I acquire that knowledge if I don't really know anyone in the industry?" AJ wondered aloud. "I don't want to look like an idiot cold calling a stranger because I don't have any base-level knowledge." AJ knew what it was like to be the least informed person on a team or a project, and it wasn't a situation he was keen to repeat.

"Books!" Harold emphasized his exclamation by pulling out a hardcover book from his own bag under the table. "This one is Mike Watson's, a guy from Utah. He was indicted because he was in real estate investing back in its heyday. In '05, '06 and '07, when the real estate market crashed, anybody who was in investment was seen as a fraud."

"I don't know if you're talking me into this…" AJ voiced sarcastically, yet in truth he was mildly alarmed. Going to jail was *not* on his vision board.

"You have to remember, indictment is not conviction," Harold said, tapping his nose. "Everyone was just reacting to the situation and felt something—anything—had to be done. Even if it was a bit overzealous.

"Anyway, Watson was able to get his ducks in a row and get all those charges to go away. But he's back at it again. In this book, *The 'Highest and Best' Real Estate Investment!*, he gives some background on the game. It's a great guide to finding investment properties and being able to buy them. I've been to numerous workshops of his and they've all been really valuable. Take this and read up."

Harold handed AJ the book and watched as AJ fit it into his messenger bag next to his vision board. AJ looked into his bag with pleasure—he was building a real estate starter kit.

"While we're on the subject of books, Robert Kiyosaki's books are what got me started," Harold mused. "I know I've referenced a few things from him already, but I have eight or nine of his books. Check out his catalog online and pick up one that interests you."

"You might also want to read some books by Dave Ramsey, even though they have nothing to do with real estate," Harold offered. "I believe in some of his philosophies, especially those relating to getting out of debt and staying out of debt. He talks about changing your priorities—replacing the BMW with paying off your home mortgage—and that luxury items aren't the things that matter. At the end of the day, what does matter is where you want to end up. I'd say ignore any advice that tells you to 'never get a home mortgage or don't use your credit card,' because as you know there's bad debt and good debt. And I don't believe in paying cash for a rental property, either. If you did that you'd be wasting the opportunity to use other people's money to generate cash flow which is the main benefit that real estate investing provides. I'm trying to shift your mindset from 'cash is king' to 'cash flow is king.' This is how you make good debt work for you. It's all about when you can buy the property and how you can leverage your money to make so much more. When it comes to real estate, his philosophies can be kind of a hindrance, but I like his general philosophies on mindset enough that I think it's still worth your time to read his stuff.

Just use discernment based on our conversations and everything else you're reading to decide what parts to keep and what parts to let go of."

It made sense to AJ, passing a blanket judgment against one broad entity—in this case, credit—seemed more like ignoring nuances rather than playing it safe. But how could he adequately assess risk if he stopped playing it safe?

#4 Talk to People About Your Idea

After refilling his cup and returning to the table, Harold returned to his keys to business success list. Luckily for AJ, the next tip addressed the concerns buzzing around his brain.

"You need to get out there and start talking to people about your idea. There's a reason think tanks exist. Ideas can be insanely good or insanely bad, but you never really know until you bounce it off of someone else."

"OK," AJ replied, still not fully satisfied by this answer. "But how do you know what people to bounce ideas off of? How do I even find these people?"

"We'll get to *where* you find them soon. First, let's focus on *who*. I surround myself with honest, intelligent people that have the same interests as me. Even better if they are smarter than I am and can teach me. I want them to think along the same lines I do, but not in exactly the same *way* I do." Harold paused. "Entrepreneurs are weird people; they are driven—they have a different level of passion than the average person. And you can feed off of that."

"And 'borrow' their ideas if they're great?"

"Definitely!" Harold clapped his hands together. "I would say most of my greatest methods came from good ol' R and D."

"What's R and D?"

"'Rip-off and Duplicate,'" he said with a laugh. "You can do that with business practices. In fact, you can do that for your personal life as well. What are other people doing to get to their first property? You don't have to do it the same exact way, but talk to other people about their methods. Take them to lunch, take them to dinner, take them out for coffee—whatever you need to do to see how they did what they did to get to that first door. Take the ideas, or parts of the ideas, that seem good to you."

"What would my first step be to find like-minded people?"

"Oh, yes, the *where*," Harold chuckled. "Meetup groups and investment groups. All you have to do is type in 'real estate investor meetups' into a search engine online and there's a local Real Estate Investment (REIA) meetup group in almost every city. That's where I would start."

"But what should I do when I get there?"

"I would recommend getting some simple business cards made, and just let people know who you are and what you want to do. Don't feel like you need to be self-conscious about being new to the game—people love to talk about themselves and their stories, and this gives them the perfect opportunity to do so. Make *them* the hero. The most important thing you can do is to simply listen, take good notes, and ask questions. You might want to craft a little elevator pitch—a short, ninety-second or less story of you and your idea and/or what you're trying to achieve."

"What would a good elevator pitch sound like for someone like me who is just starting out? Saying I'm trying to get, you know, twenty-five doors or something?"

"At first, it may be just that. Something like, 'Hey, my goal is to get to twenty-five doors. I want to be doing this full-time before I retire, which is ten years or thirty years—whenever that is—from now.' Let people know what your down-the-road goal is and see who can help you get to that point—whether it's them or someone they know."

"All of the connections you make become incredibly important as you start your new business. Ask all of your connections for referrals—both for services you need and for your own services as aid to others. Be sure to thank everyone that refers anyone to you in any capacity. See if there's anything you can do for them. Make sure they know you're appreciative, and keep a good name out there for yourself—don't just be a 'taker.'"

"What are some ways I can give back if I don't have a lot of services to leverage right away?"

"Pay for their coffee, pay for the breakfast, pay for the lunch," Harold suggested. "Remember, you're interrupting them and their lives to gather information when you invite them out. I don't expect you to do that here since this is essentially my away-from-home office and I'd be here anyway."

"Are there any networking services or mentorships I should pay for?"

"With real estate knowledge, I don't want people to spend a whole lot of money at the get-go. Especially when there are so many hands being held out in real estate saying, 'Oh, I can help you with this—just give me $15,000.' Or, 'Hey, I'll teach you how to do that for only $30,000.' You'll get more value out of your own networking and connection-creating than giving money away to formal training opportunities or programs.

"Go to the meetups to find first-hand education and get referrals. Be realistic—if it smells too good to be true, it probably is. Carefully vet every paid seminar before you shell out the cash and see if you're getting any bonuses out of the deal. I went to a free real estate investing workshop once, where they then upsold people into a three-day seminar for $497 that came with an inch and a half manual and a couple of DVDs. The manual was full of excellent advice—almost worth more than the seminar itself. I knew once I got to the three-day seminar they'd be trying to sell me into their $15-30k training program, which I couldn't afford and didn't want to do. I made it very clear to myself and others while I was there I was only investing in the three-day seminar and nothing else. I squeezed every last drop out of the information they provided while I was there, and

I asked every mentor onsite a ton of questions and really got my money's worth. I then went home and studied the manual like crazy, and learned a ton more. So few people do that; most people just get sucked in to the next biggest and best thing before exhausting, digesting and executing on the information they already have right in front of them. If people you get to know at a meetup ask you to go to a class or seminar, start asking around to see if others have attended and if it benefited them. Talk to past attendees before you go to any new type of learning program to see how valuable it really is. Read the reviews. Do your homework before you commit."

"Is there any cap on the amount you would spend for a seminar or class?"

"I wouldn't spend more than $1,000 on any single event. Honestly, you can go to YouTube University for free, if you know what I mean. There's so much free information you can get on there by following people's channels and asking questions. I tell my kids I'd personally rather have them go to YouTube University and be an entrepreneur and get into their own business than I would have them go to a college for a four-year business degree."

"Really? A crowdsourced internet education over an accredited one?" AJ laughed.

"For me, yes. I wish I had that resource eighteen years ago," Harold replied without any irony. "I would have eaten that up, but it just wasn't around like it is today. It's a better fit for my learning style. But you *do* need to be cautious. When you hear conflicting information online from different experts, be sure to write it down, formulate questions about the discordant details, and take them to a mentor. You'll get a lot of different opinions in the online world you can take to mentors in the offline world to verify or refute. This is part of your research. Don't just learn from one person and have that be the gospel by which you make all of your decisions. There's a thousand different ways to do business, you just have to find the method that works best for you."

"And after you think you've honed in on a method that meshes with your research?"

"Then you have to take the leap of faith and jump in," Harold said with a grin. "There's only so much theoretical work you can do before you just have to take action and do it. Trial by error is sometimes the only way to discover what works best."

#5 Take Action

"That sounds… horrifying," AJ replied.

"Fear can be one of the best motivators," Harold countered. "If you're afraid, you want to work from that fear. The only way to get out of that state of terror is by finding the right method—the way that works."

"But if you haven't discovered it from books or mentors, how do you do that?"

"Look in places you normally wouldn't, and do things you normally wouldn't. Leave no stone unturned—put into practice all of the information and methods you've collected theoretically. If one method doesn't work, try another. I do things I normally wouldn't do if I think it will prove successful. The ultimate goal is to make sure I can find a method to make success happen. Which leads to the next important tip—almost more important than this one."

'Take action' struck AJ as a pretty important tip, considering you could talk about plans all day, but nothing would actually happen until you enacted them. What could be more important than that?

#6 Don't Give Up

"This may seem like a no-brainer to you, but don't give up," Harold paused and AJ wondered if it was meant for dramatic effect or just a natural rest. Either way, it was dramatic. "I can't tell you how many times I've seen someone hit their first roadblock and just quit.

"Endure. Persevere. Hang in there. Real estate is a cycle and, as such, has its ups and downs. Don't give up. If a wall comes up, go around it or tear it down."

"Even if you start losing money?"

"AJ, I'll tell you, when I started out with a plumbing business and lost money in it, I got an even stronger desire for cash flow and a different style of operating. If it wasn't for that experience, I don't think I'd have been able to persevere when I opened my own franchises in a different industry. Adversity is one of the best teachers."

After pondering for a moment, AJ then responded, "I feel like there's a difference between 'adversity' and 'failing.'"

"My property management franchise only exists because of the failings I experienced with my plumbing business," Harold replied slowly. "I wanted to build something that allowed me to be anywhere in the world. Something without a day-to-day component that required me to be in-office. The plumbing business taught me that about myself.

"People may tell you to give up. I had people telling me that what I wanted to do wouldn't be profitable. But then I looked at competitors out there. I was doing the exact same thing they were doing, but I had to do it better and find a way to separate my business from the competition."

"I guess that's why market research is so important?" AJ offered. "And staying up on your competitors and the industry as a whole?"

"Exactly," Harold replied with pride. "I knew I had a better product, a better image, better branding. I felt like I was building a better business than my competitors, and today, five years later, I can see I was right. Look where we are, where our competitors are, and then give it another five years. We're going to be miles apart from them. Don't give up; you'll carve out your spot in the marketplace as something different that fulfills a need people didn't know they had."

A moment of silence passed between the pair as Harold watched AJ making more notes. After he had finished writing, AJ tapped his pen on the pad three times in thought—would everyone be against him?

"It sounds like a lot to tackle on your own," AJ said.

"That brings us to our next tip, AJ," Harold said as he interlaced his hands and leaned forward.

#7 Have a Support System

"As you may well know, setbacks are a part of business and there's no way around that fact. Life is going to throw you obstacles. Things just happen. Have a support system to lean on—which may not be your family—you may have to go outside for support. Fortunately, I didn't have to."

Harold retrieved a photo from his wallet and handed it to AJ. A woman, roughly Harold's age, smiled back at him from the small, square frame.

"You can't give up. You need to have a support system that will help to prop you back up if you even start *thinking* about quitting. I've been there and done that, and I tend to rely on my wife as my support system. But remember, it doesn't always have to be family."

Taking a moment to smile warmly at the photo before tucking it back into his wallet, Harold retained that warmness when he fixed his gaze on AJ once more.

"What type of things would she say or do?" AJ asked, mesmerized by the instant change the photo created in Harold's demeanor.

"She would remind me of things I had said to her a year ago." Harold paused for what AJ assumed was a fond recollection. "Or she'd repeat what I had previously described as my vision. Those reminders propped me back up. Then I'd think, 'Oh yeah, I can do that. It just may take a little longer than I had expected.'"

Nodding, AJ thought of his support system—mostly friends and nearby cousins he knew would always answer his phone calls, or commiserate with him. Even Pete crossed his mind as a viable option. Harold was right; it could be anyone as long as he trusted them.

#8 Navigate the Naysayers

"The next one," Harold began, "comes back to the mindset you've trained yourself to have. Don't allow your brain to entertain negativity. Navigate the naysayers by teaching yourself to be able to forget and let the negativity go."

"But what if it is a persistent problem in your life from someone you can't cut off contact with? Like a parent or sibling?" AJ asked, thinking of his relatively unsupportive parents who had always championed the traditional college route.

"That can be tricky," Harold admitted. "At one point, one of my business partners was getting people he knew to come on board on his side. We would go meet with them and they'd say things like, 'Oh, well, if I were you, I would close this business down and just forget about it.' The business was $300,000 in debt at this point."

"That *is* quite a lot to be in the hole," AJ conceded.

"But it was all my money sunk into it!" Harold exclaimed. "I couldn't just walk away. That wasn't an option, and naysaying any productive ideas was not beneficial to the situation. My best bet was to let my partner deal with those people and just continue with my plans separately."

"And that's just part of starting your own business. If you're going into any type of business, your first two years are the worst. Maybe even three. Survive those first two, when you may not even get a paycheck, and you'll pull through. You've got to get through that period. It goes back to perseverance."

Silently, AJ was congratulating himself for signing up to drive for the ridesharing apps—even if his business didn't take off right away, he'd have the certainty of some backup income at the very least.

"Train your brain to forget about negativity and the discouraging things other people say. Our minds are the most powerful things in the world. For example, once I hop on a plane, I go to sleep. For the first five years, I could never do it. But then I reasoned with myself, 'I can't do anything on this plane. What am I going to do? The most productive thing I could do is catch up on sleep.'"

"Did it work?"

"You bet. Once again, the mind is a powerful thing, and if you can train it or reason with it, you're set. Think of your mind as precious real estate and you don't want any negativity occupying that space. Save the land in your head for your motivators."

#9 Keep Your Eye on the Prize

"Speaking of motivators, you'll need to continually revisit your 'Why.'"

AJ tried to guess where Harold was going with this. "To rework it?"

"That may come into play eventually, but remembering what spurred your ambition in the first place, and what you have to look forward to after all of your hard work, will keep you motivated to keep going.

"Sometimes I'll take a long look at some of the things people are saying and wonder, 'Am I not seeing what other people are seeing? Should I really close? Should I really be done with this business? Should I move on to a different business?'"

"Doesn't that go back to navigating the naysayers?"

"It does. But when this type of talk is coming from your trusted advisors or business partners, I think you should take a step back and reevaluate it," Harold tapped his head to indicate thinking critically. "These people may be telling you something in this instance. It can be a good idea to close a business depending on what's going on. Remembering your long-term goal and evaluating your situation against the trajectory to reach it is valuable.

"You have to be alert and acknowledge the signals. Learn to differentiate between naysayers, and the valuable perspectives from trusted sources who may be able to see your current situation and long-term goal more clearly from the outside."

#10 Be Patient

"Probably the most important tip that lays the foundation for all of the others is to be patient."

AJ chortled and said, "I think that's the one I'll have the most issues with."

"Remember, AJ, there's no such thing as an overnight success," Harold cautioned. "You need to go all in, work hard, and be patient. Amazon, Apple—all of these big name companies—weren't overnight successes. People exaggerate and claim they were, but they had really been hard at work for upwards of fifteen years by the point they really hit their stride. Apple even went through a rebrand. Everyone seems to forget they started out as Macintosh."

"Really? I've never even heard that before. They were actually called Macintosh before?" AJ replied, aghast. "So that's why it's called a 'Mac' now. Ha! Got it."

"That little tidbit of trivia might be aging me. I forget how young you are." Harold shook his head and chuckled. "But the point I'm making is, none of this is a get-rich-quick scheme. Creating cash flow is, for most people, just like retirement—it's slow and steady. But just like retirement, it's security. As long as you buy real estate with the end in mind—the idea that you're going to be playing the long game—you'll do fine. It's when people aren't patient and want instant gratification that things go awry."

"So, I shouldn't panic and sell if a property drops down in value?"

"That's the worst thing you can do," Harold warned, "because real estate is a cycle. You may have a property worth half of what you originally bought it for, but continue to wait it out. You make your money when you buy. Be patient—it'll pick back up. In fact, if prices drop dramatically and you have the cash flow in place, pick up another property! Warren Buffet became one of the wealthiest men in the world by buying stocks when they plunged really low and not letting them go.

"Once you have cash flow coming from an initial property, you can use that cash to invest in more properties and create more cash flow. Which brings us to your homework this time: you have some theoretical guidance, now it's time to go and research some properties so we can talk specifics and start to give you some practical tactics."

———————

With Harold's ten keys to business success both on his mind and written in the notepad beside him, AJ took to the internet to research investment properties in what he hoped was his price range. He knew he would probably have to take out an investment loan (but reminded himself this was good debt, not bad). AJ chose geographic locations to investigate based on previous considerations Harold had mentioned—in locations that would either be easy for him to get to, or ones he wouldn't mind spending time in and could justify the price of a plane ticket as a dual investment in his business and his own travel pleasure.

Thus, AJ embarked on his first practical step on his road to making cash flow work for him.

ACTION ITEMS:

1. Watch Simon Sinek's TED Talk, "How Great Leaders Inspire Action." This seventeen-and-a-half-minute long video will walk you through the importance of starting with your "why."

2. Write out your financial goal and reverse engineer how many doors you will need to hit that number.

3. Start researching potential investment properties just to get a sense of prices, what's out there, and becoming familiar with different websites and the way properties are listed.

BEST PRACTICE:
Once you know what your area of focus is, become a student of that craft. Read books, listen to podcasts, and attend seminars, programs and events. Take in as much knowledge as you can.

CHAPTER SIX
TRUST YOUR GUT

Always trust your gut. It knows what
your head hasn't figured out yet.
Unknown

It had been a couple of weeks since AJ first started meeting Harold at the little downtown café. Even if AJ hadn't been keeping track of his progress by way of his homework, the staff's familiarity toward him at the café would have been an indicator. The young woman who had rung him up during almost every visit greeted him again today—by name—with a warm, "Good to see you, AJ."

When AJ joined Harold with his shortlist of researched properties, he had one burning question.

"How do you know which properties to buy and which to let go of?"

"Honestly, there's no specific formula to decide that," Harold smiled sadly. "You can't train for it. It's a gut feeling that comes with time and that trial and error factor I mentioned before.

"But don't just think I mean something airy-fairy when I say a gut feeling. It's not just a blind hunch. Your subconscious is far more powerful than your conscious mind, AJ. As humans we are constantly exposed to thousands of tiny, microscopic details coming at us every second of every day, and our subconscious minds are always working to collect, retain and sort that data behind-the-scenes—whether we realize it or not. When you have a gut feeling, your subconscious is communicating with you. Your gut is saying to you that it's been collecting and working with this data and based on its assimilation of the data against the problem at hand, this is the probable answer—which is usually an intuitive feeling that is either generally classified as a positive feeling, or a negative one.

"These gut feelings aren't random, and they can't happen without having adequate technical knowledge about a subject. You have to do your homework, and be exposed to the data in order for it all to come together at the right moment—when it's time to make a decision. Without that, it's not a gut feeling, it's a guess. It's roulette. And it's highly irresponsible.

"With my plumbing business, I started sensing things were amiss and it was only when I started having a strong gut feeling it wasn't working out that I finally conceded I wasn't on the right path. First, I tried changing course a little bit—that's part of sticking with it, which you should always do initially. Try to make it work. But when things in that situation weren't changing, I knew I had to bail. I stand by that old adage, 'If you're going to fail, fail fast.'

"A real estate example I can give you happened with one of my friend Nick's protégés. The mentee sold his house in California to buy some investment properties. He brought his shortlist to Nick, much like you have done with me, for a second opinion. Nick looked it over and he had a negative gut feeling about them. He'd been in the business awhile and had seen what happens with properties with similar characteristics to the ones his student was considering. That gut feeling was based on experience: it was cultivated over time and with exposure. To help speed up that process, you need to educate yourself, do your homework, and consult professionals until you become a professional yourself."

"I was looking at these with the idea of having them be rentals—maybe even vacation rentals," AJ said, somewhat hesitantly.

Harold perused the list. AJ could tell he was mentally noting the locations of each. Harold pulled out a pen and started making notes next to each, but AJ couldn't make out what he was writing.

"Learn and investigate what makes a good rental property and what doesn't," Harold advised. "Educate yourself on the market and the conditions of each city. For vacation rentals, you want to be sure your chosen city has an adequate amount of tourist attractions or incoming visitors to warrant going that route. Additionally, you need to be sure that your chosen city allows for nightly rentals and find out what the minimum and maximum rental periods are. You don't want to buy a vacation property and then be unable to rent it out because of city ordinances."

"I actually considered both of those things when looking at each of these. I was trying to make an informed decision."

"Excellent work," Harold said as he nodded in approval.

"How long did it take you to cultivate a gut feeling? In your real estate history, what would you do differently if you could?"

"If I could do my real estate career over," Harold imagined with a laugh, "I would get on a real estate team, be trained and mentored by the team lead, bust my butt and work there for two years and then leave. I'd consider it my crash course in real estate. A paid internship."

"But when you left, wouldn't that person be totally pissed off?"

"Oh, my, yes," Harold assented. "That's why what I did was a more amiable way of going about it. I partnered with someone to show me the ropes and I financially backed my investment with money I had accrued to pull my own weight. He brought his knowledge and institutions, and I took on good debt to acquire equity. But if you're asking what I would do over again, the point isn't just to join a team for joining a team's sake—it actually has really very little to do with being on a team, per se. The point is there's such incredible value in both education and experience—a team typically just has ample helpings of both. And as you get started, you need to find the best possible vehicle to give you those two things. You don't need to go into a team environment to do that, however—especially these days with the volume of courses, programs, videos, podcasts, eBooks and training tools that are available both on and offline—but you *do* need to invest time and energy into becoming an expert in your field.

"Another important way to gain both education and experience is through a relationship with a mentor," Harold continued. "You've already nailed that part—with a great choice, I might add," he said with a chuckle. "But as you grow in your career, through the various meetups you go to and as you expand your network, you will always want to look for new and different mentors who have very specific areas of expertise so they can help you navigate the waters as you fine tune your area of interest further within the umbrella of real estate investing. For example, I personally like to have friends and mentors who are in the legal field," he said wisely. "You never know what's just around the corner and it certainly doesn't hurt to have a stacked deck of people who can help in a crisis if ever the need arose."

AJ nodded and thought to himself, *Trusting your gut isn't nearly as woo-woo as it sounds. It's actually a combination of education and experience coming together in the background, giving you feedback as you look at a new situation. It's pretty amazing, actually, that the human brain and body can process so much so quickly behind the scenes. Once I graduated I thought I was done with all that studying, but I guess I'm going to have to do a LOT more of it in this next phase!*

ACTION ITEMS:

1. Educate yourself on the market you wish to invest in so you can make informed decisions. Consider things like city ordinances, tourist attractions and events (particularly important if you are purchasing a vacation rental), rental cycles, public safety, etc.

2. Get a mentor and look for opportunities to gain experience in your field in a short amount of time, using other people's knowledge to shorten the learning curve and eliminate making the same mistakes others have already made and are willing to share with you.

BEST PRACTICE:
Dig your well before you're thirsty: always be thinking ahead to potential challenges, and start building relationships with people who could provide support or assistance when you're in need.

CHAPTER SEVEN
GETTING STARTED

A little action often spurs a lot of momentum.
Noah Scalin

AJ left his shortlist with Harold as he approached the counter again for a refill. Behind the register was the same woman who had remembered his name—and despite the length of time he and Harold had been there, she was still on shift.

"Long day?" AJ asked her.

"I was just promoted to General Manager. It's salary-based, which means I'm here indefinitely." She laughed good-naturedly and AJ enjoyed the light, lyrical laugh—it reminded him of wind chimes.

When AJ returned to the table, Harold was ready for him.

"All of your shortlist properties are solid, so now you'll want to go and look at them in person. You won't continue to do this throughout your career, because the data will be able to tell you everything you need to know, but it's definitely helpful when you're first getting started to go and look at both the properties you're targeting that are for sale, as well as ones in the area that have recently sold. Most of the ones you've listed here are in the vicinity, and the rest are weekend trips.

"One thing most people don't get with real estate is that it's a business." Harold looked serious. "Treating your real estate business like a true business means creating a business entity, creating bank accounts in the name of the LLC, and making sure you set aside money to reinvest in cash flow. You've already done the entity-formation part, but now let's talk about the day-to-day banking element. When it comes to having rental properties, you'll want to have two separate business bank accounts to start: one checking and one savings. The money that comes in from the business, called revenue, goes into the checking account and you will also pay the basic monthly expenses from this account. The savings account will hold your slush fund."

"My what?" AJ asked, confused.

"When you have a business, you need to have a buffer. Things happen."

"What types of things, for example?"

"A water heater goes out or the furnace quits working, etc. Things the landlord would figure out for a renter—but now *you're* the landlord. If you have a buffer, that doesn't become a problem. I'd recommend $1,000 to $2,500 per property depending on its age and condition. Hold that buffer, along with the security deposits for each tenant, in your business savings account or 'slush fund.' This way, by keeping the savings account slush fund separate you're never short on money for repairs or returning your tenant's security deposit on time. You always know exactly how much you have to fix the property whenever something goes wrong, and you aren't taking funds away from yourself or your family if there's a gap between when a tenant moves out and needs their deposit and another one moves in and pays the new one. There are legalities around the timeline for returning a tenant's security deposit to them, so you have to make sure you have the cash to be able to fulfill your legal obligation to return it on time."

"OK, got it," AJ said, beginning to understand.

"Then, after all of your business expenses are paid from your business checking account, you can take the excess profit and transfer it to your personal account to use however you'd like. That's personal income. Or you can determine a set amount per month and set it up as an auto transfer from your business account to your personal account, so it'll feel like you're getting a regular paycheck again."

"How much excess do you tend to have and what do you do with it?"

"I mentioned before that my wife and I will take a weekend trip to explore a new city," Harold recalled as a pleasant smile overtook his face. "But, outside of that, I tend to just put the cash away in savings or reinvest it. If you aren't looking to reinvest or create more cash flow, a personal savings account is fine, or another investment vehicle. Just make sure you understand how liquid your money is and if there are any penalties or fees to pull your money out if you find a great deal you want to invest in.

"Some people treat real estate investing as if it's passive income they can use indiscriminately. They confuse revenue with income and will often think, 'I have $500 or $1,000 from our rental, let's go spend it—let's go to Disneyland!' But there's a very big difference between the revenue your business generates, the monthly expenses you have to pay out, slush fund and emergency expenses, and your personal income. So let's talk about income more specifically."

"Remember when I drew out Kiyosaki's Cashflow Quadrant for you back at one of our earlier meetings, and we talked about active income versus passive income?"

"Yes," said AJ, "It was part of our cash *flow* is king conversation, which you said was the single most important thing I needed to take away from our time together."

"Correct!" said Harold.

AJ could tell that Harold loved it when his protégés really paid attention and could access his teachings on the fly. He imagined how it must make him feel like his time was being well spent, and that he was truly making a difference in their lives.

Harold continued, "Well, I only taught you about active and passive income, but there are actually *three* types of income:

active income (sometimes called earned income), passive income, and portfolio income.

"Active, or earned income, is just that—income you *earn*. You have to actively participate in the earning of this type of income. One form of earned income in the real estate investment field would be when you personally remodel or rehab a property with the intention of improving it and thereby increasing the value to then turn around and sell it at a higher price."

"Ahhh, clever," AJ said with a wry smile. *Funny how self-explanatory some words can be once you learn what they mean,* he thought. *Active, or earned income—it seems so obvious now.*

Harold continued, hammering the point home even further, "Passive income, on the other hand, is also just that—it's *passive.* You can sit back and not need to do any more deals and the money will continue to roll in week after week, month after month. In general business terms, we call this kind of income 'MRR' or 'Monthly Recurring Revenue,' and it's an incredibly important element in creating a higher valuation for your company if you want to sell it down the road as this demonstrates the regular income potential from your entire portfolio. In real estate specifically, this recurring revenue, or passive income, would come from your 'buy and hold' properties—your leases and rentals, where the tenants pay rent every month on a recurring basis for the term of the lease. Do you see the genius in passive income yet?" Harold asked, beaming. It was so obvious how passionately excited he was about the concept, and his enthusiasm was contagious.

"Heck, yeah, I do!" exclaimed AJ. "It's unbelievable! Now I finally understand how the rich keep getting richer. It's like a merry-go-round in a playground; once it gets going, it gets easier to keep it going with less effort. With every new property it just keeps getting better and better, and the cash flow just keeps rolling in month after month! Cash flow really IS KING!!! I get it, I get it! I really actually get it!" By this point, AJ was practically shouting with excitement.

Harold let out a booming laugh, causing the other patrons in the coffee shop to glance over at their table to see what was going on.

"All right, kid, great breakthrough. But let's not stop here. In real estate investing, your passive income options are rentals (which we've already talked about), something called lease options, recreational parks (where you rent out spaces), mobile home parks (where you rent out lots and other people own the mobile homes themselves), commercial spaces (offices, retail, storage unit facilities, industrial buildings, etc.), and property management.

"With property management, you can manage your properties yourself, or you can outsource it and hire a property management company to do it for you. But remember—just as you can hire a property management *company* to collect rent payments for you, other investors hire people and companies to collect rent payments for them, too, and they pay a fee or a percentage of rents each month to a property management company for that service. So, you can do what I did and start a company that offers property management, and build an additional passive income stream doing that for other people.

"Even though we've already talked about rentals, deserving of special mention in that category before we move on is one of my favorites—apartments. Any guesses why I like apartment buildings, AJ?"

"Yes," AJ said proudly. "Because you buy one building, but then rent each individual door by the month and collect multiple rent payments every month but only have one structure to deal with and maintain."

"Bingo."

"So what we've been talking about are 'buy and hold' properties. They're part of a long-term wealth generation strategy where you'll benefit from appreciation, equity and tax advantages while also generating passive income cash flow on a recurring monthly basis. But there are other streams of active (or earned income) that will help you generate larger amounts of cash more quickly and move toward acquiring buy and hold properties in due time. Right now, since you're just getting started, you'll need to push the merry-go-round to get it going. It's going to take some effort and work. So let's look at your options for income streams within the active income or earned income category so you can start making money *now*."

Having seen the proverbial light, AJ was grateful to now be turning their attention back to tactics and advice he could put to use today. He was eager to roll up his sleeves and choose a path within what he could now see was a much larger world of real estate investing than he had initially realized existed. And the thought of earning money sooner rather than later appealed to him immensely.

"For active income generation in real estate, you've got a few options. I've taken the liberty of making a list to at least get you started, so you can go home and research each one individually," Harold said as he slid a list across the table.

It read:

EARNED/ACTIVE INCOME STREAMS IN REAL ESTATE

- Wholesaling (Contract Sales)
- Pre-foreclosures, Foreclosures, and Real Estate Owned Properties (Post-foreclosures)
- Probate
- Discount Note Selling
- Land Development
- Remodeling
- Rehabbing

"Go home, and go through them one by one. Watch videos online, look up the definitions of each term, and pay attention to how you feel when you're learning about them. Put a star beside any that feel like they resonate with you, and before we meet again I want you to narrow it down to only one so we have a concrete place to get started."

ACTION ITEMS:

1. Set up a business checking account in the name of your LLC, plus a savings account to hold your buffer and slush fund as well as your security deposit(s).

2. Investigate the list of active or earned income streams from Harold's list above, and determine which stream you'd like to tackle first.

BEST PRACTICE:
Don't confuse your revenue with your income. Make sure you always keep adequate funds in your slush fund account to cover repairs as well as security deposits.

CHAPTER EIGHT
OTHER PEOPLE'S MONEY

I love money more than the things it can buy...but what
I love more than money is other people's money.
Danny DeVito
as Lawrence Garfield in the 1991 movie Other People's Money

AJ found the process of going through the types of earned income streams relatively easy once he got into it. Learning about each one individually and then paying attention to how he felt, as Harold had suggested, led to a definitive, and fairly quick, conclusion.

"Rehabbing," he said as he sat down.

"I'm clear, and I've made my decision. It's rehabbing," he repeated.

"Great!" said Harold. "Then let's dive right in. Since we were talking about active, earned income streams, I assume you'll be rehabbing for a fix and flip, right?"

"Yes. Based on our prior conversation and the research I've done, I definitely want to get into the buy and hold game as a long-term passive income strategy, but I think to try to get the merry go round spinning as quickly as I can, I should consider doing a couple of fix and flips in the short term to generate some cash, shouldn't I?"

"Yes—that will definitely give you some momentum and get things moving."

"I'm pretty sure I already know the answer to this, but have you ever done any fix and flips before?" AJ wondered if his question would come across as offensive to such an established investor as Harold.

"I sure have! I've done probably twenty to twenty-five of them, most of which I bought on the county auction steps. That method's become very, very competitive—not just here in Utah, but all across the country. I remember in the late 90's and the early 2000's going down to the county steps—here in Utah, the auctions are usually Tuesdays, Wednesdays or Thursdays—and getting eaten alive as a newbie investor. You see, there's a group of 'Old Timers' who go to Denny's or the Village Inn beforehand, for coffee and breakfast, and—like a bunch of sports team owners making trades right before the draft—they're asking each other, *'Hey, what properties do you want?' 'I was going to bid on this. You can take this one and I'll take this one,'* so they don't outbid each other. Fast forward to around '07-'08, and the Old Timers were still there, though slowly but surely a few newbies like me were starting to try to make a move. But you've got to understand, AJ, as a newbie I learned that you gotta pay your dues before the Old Timers are going to let you in. And it's not going to be easy, they're going to make your life *rough*. '*Oh, you want this house?*' They'll bid it up high and they don't care who gets it. If they get it for $30,000 over asking price, that's fine to them—just as long as you didn't get it. If you ended up bidding it up and it's $20,000-30,000 more than they want, they'll be laughing and thinking, '*Go for it. Let's see if you can make a profit on that.*' They want you to buy it, leave, and they hope to never see you again because you bought way too high and weren't able to make a dollar. Or you lost money on it, or you spent all of your money on that one property so you're not going to come back.

"So… you almost need to have an Old Timer in your network as an inside track to even get a property that way these days. When I buy at the county steps, I use a buyer. The Old Timers have set it up so that I pay them a thousand dollars for a successful bid. I have to give them a $20,000 cashiers check up front just to get them to bid for me, and then I have to give them the rest of the money in cash within twenty-four hours. So the Old Timers are making money off all of us who want to buy at the county steps, but at least it's a way in. If you're not in their circle, they're going to make life hell for you if you try to get in.

"Now I look for distressed properties or distressed sellers—or even better, both!"

"Distressed sellers? What?! Why are you looking for sellers who are in distress?" Alarm bells were going off in AJ's head. After all this time and feeling like he really knew his mentor, he couldn't believe he was hearing Harold speak of a strategy where he intentionally was preying upon people who were down on their luck. It just didn't seem like him at all, and it made him extremely nervous.

"It's not exactly what you think it is, AJ. At least not the way *I* do these deals, anyways. Distressed sellers have a need, and—as you know—I absolutely love helping people. I love talking to them and hearing their stories and understanding what their needs and desires are to see how I can make an honest deal happen to create a win-win for both of us. Let me give you an example. I met a guy who had cancer, and he really needed money. I was honest and up front with him, and told him if he could wait two months, we would list his property 'as is' at a discount of 5% and he would be able to make $65,000— maybe $75,000. He was so overwhelmed and just wanted to get out as soon as he could financially, because he just couldn't deal with the stress emotionally. He just needed cash. There are so many people who would have preyed upon a guy like that, who wouldn't have educated him on how these things work and who wouldn't have given him the option to wait it out and get more—they'd have just taken it for themselves and would have been cutthroat and dishonest. Our industry sometimes gets a bad rap, and I think it's oftentimes because of investors like that. To me, partnering with sellers and supporting them to get what they need creates a human element inside what is otherwise often just a transactional business.

"In this particular situation, when the guy saw the cards laid out in front of him honestly, he was able to make an informed decision that he ultimately felt was right for him and his family, and he was able to choose to get his equity out up front in a quick, clean cash deal without regret. Often in these scenarios, if the possibilities haven't been properly explained to the seller, they end up seeing the flip side of the deal later, and they are filled with bitterness and regret and feel like they've been scammed. If only they'd have known to wait two months they could have made significantly more than what they walked away with. And when someone is already in distress, layering that extra level of regret upon them is just heartless. So I like to have real, transparent conversations with people and allow them to make choices based on having all of the information. They are in control of making whatever decision is right for them, and together we create a deal that gives benefit to both parties yet still allows the seller to be in the driver's seat and make the final call.

"So that's an example of a distressed seller. Now let's talk about the distressed property/distressed seller combination.

"I own a website called WeBuyHomesUtah.com, and this lady contacted us through the site. I went and saw the property and then asked my contractor to go out to the house and check on it. It was the middle of the winter—probably negative five or even negative ten degrees outside—and a pipe on the exterior of the house froze and burst, flooding it. When my contractor arrived the water was still running. He was able to get the water turned off, but there was a ton of damage. I was already planning to replace the carpet and the kitchen floor, and paint—and do a lot of those types of high-value fixes—if I was able to buy the property but at the end of the day I was able to get the property for $30,000 less and the owner's insurance company paid her the difference. The mitigation team cut into the walls about two feet high, and took the trim off and dried it all out. So I ended up having to pay a little bit more because I had to repair the damage, but in the end I made more because of the discounted sale price than what I'd have made before.

"I prefer buying properties directly from the owner(s) versus ones that are listed on the MLS, because there is a great opportunity when working with the owner directly for something called seller financing."

AJ drew in a long, deep breath. He always felt like a fish out of water whenever the subject of money came up, and the topic of financing seemed no different—finance, financial, financing—it was definitely all related to money.

Harold continued, not stopping for even a moment. "Let's talk about one of my very favorite topics: OPM," Harold said, his eyes twinkling and a mischievous look curling the corners of his lips.

"OPM?" AJ asked, trying to figure out what the acronym might stand for on his own. "Operating Principles for Management?" he said, giving it a shot in the dark guess.

"No, but I love that you're not afraid to try guessing when you have no idea of the answer! Nice one. That in itself is great progress, AJ. Being willing to fail is an absolute criteria for success. In this case, OPM stands for Other People's Money."

"Ahhhh," AJ said with a smile. *I wasn't even close*, he thought with a laugh.

"Other People's Money is a very important concept to grasp when it comes to investing," Harold began. "It's a slang term that refers to financial leverage (or borrowed capital) used to increase the potential returns (as well as the risks) of an investment. Credit and OPM are the keys to creating your fortune, AJ, and if you borrow right, you will make money. It's the 'good debt' we talked about before.

"In real estate, there are six main types of OPM," he said as he held up his fingers one by one, listing them out, "Banks, private lenders—which are sometimes called 'hard money lenders', seller financing—sometimes called a 'seller carryback,' investors, government tax credits, and cash flow from operations."

AJ struggled to write fast enough to capture all six. "Let me make sure I got them all: banks, hard money lenders, seller financing, investors, government tax credits, and cash flow from operations. Is that correct?"

"Yes," Harold said, appreciative that his student cared so much about getting things right.

"I'm going to give you a very brief overview on each one now, but in the coming weeks you'll want to take the time to research all six on your own to fully understand your options for financing.

"Let's start with the traditional route: banks. Generally, with a single-family home, a bank will cover up to 80% of a home's value and you will cover the other 20%. But for first-time homebuyers, there is something called a Federal Housing Administration (FHA) loan, which can cover up to 96.5% of the purchase price with the buyer only having to kick in the other 3.5% if you have a credit score of at least 580. If your credit score is between 500 and 579, you can still get an FHA loan provided you can come up with a 10% down payment. By comparison, you'll typically need a credit score of at least 620 and a down payment between 3% and 20% to qualify for a conventional mortgage. What's your credit score?"

"Ummm, I don't know," AJ replied sheepishly. "I'm embarrassed to say that I actually have no idea where I'm at."

"Credit is a powerful tool that people who are 'wealth builders' use to get wealthier," Harold said, a frown forming on his forehead for the first time in any meeting he had had with his protégé. "We'll talk about this at our next meeting in detail, but for now just know that it's a really important part of your overall strategy.

"Now… where were we before we got sidetracked?" Harold said out loud, mostly to himself. "Ahhh, yes. FHA loans. There are owner occupancy rules you have to pay attention to with FHA loans; they require that you live in the property as your primary residence for a specific length of time after the loan closes. So you'll want to research and consider whether or not this is the right option for you, because it ultimately may not be." AJ nodded, encouraging Harold to continue. "You'll also want to make sure, in addition to the money you'll have to put down, that you have the money you need for any repairs you want to make to the property. You could also use other banking products to act as OPM to cover any short-term repairs or fixes, like your existing line of credit. You could try to open a credit card strictly for your business to cover any of those expenses, too—but to do that you're going to need a couple of years' financials to apply for one. No matter which vehicle you choose, however, you've got to be disciplined and use it responsibly so you don't get yourself in trouble."

He sounds like my dad, AJ thought. *Except I know for sure my dad doesn't know this kind of stuff. But it's good advice, I guess—even if it is old school.*

"Next we have private loans/hard money lenders," Harold's voice jolted AJ back to reality and the conversation at hand. "There are private lenders and equity firms, angel funds, investment groups, and many institutions out there who are looking for good investments to put money into. These loans will often be more expensive with higher interest rates, so you'll want to be careful and navigate this option mindfully."

"Then there's seller financing. This is when the seller of a property acts as a lender for all or part of the property. It might be at market rate or could even be higher depending on the risk. Sometimes the seller wants to take part in a portion of the profit in exchange for both a lower rate and you doing all of the work and management of the property."

"OK, wait. Back up a second." AJ looked confused. "Did you say this was when the seller of the property acts as the *lender?*"

"Yes, that's right."

"I don't get it," AJ confessed, clearly missing something. "If someone is selling a property, doesn't that mean they want out of it? Why on earth would a person want to do that when they're trying to sell?"

"They may just be tired of all the work required to run the property," Harold offered up. "Or they could be looking for a more stable return from collecting a set interest amount on their money instead of navigating the ups and downs of rental income. This strategy has the potential to earn better rates on their money than they would from investing that same sum of money other ways. There's also a potential for a lump-sum option where the promissory note can be sold to an investor to get an up front payment right away. Another reason might be that they want to sell their property 'as is' and not have to do a bunch of expensive repairs. With seller financing you can do this, without having to make all of the costly fixes that traditional lenders may require. Not only that, it's potentially faster to close the deal, since the buyers avoid the mortgage process altogether. You pay the mortgage and the insurance, fix it up using your own money, and then when it sells, the mortgage is paid off and everyone is clear. Last but not least, there's risk protection to some degree—the seller gets to retain title on the property, AND if the buyer defaults, they keep the down payment and any money that was paid, *in addition to* the property itself."

"What?! That's crazy," AJ said, "I had no idea that was even a thing. What sounded ridiculous at the beginning actually sounds like a pretty good deal for someone if the situation was right. Who knew," he said, shaking his head and laughing. "I have *so* much to learn."

"There are a couple of nuances you need to make sure are handled properly with seller financing—one of which is insurance," Harold said with a twinge of something in his voice AJ couldn't quite put his finger on. "I got lucky once with a seller financing deal I was doing, where there ended up being a flood on the property. Sometimes what happens is the owner thinks because they've 'sold' the property to someone else, they'll cancel the insurance to reduce their expenses. *No, no, no, no, no, no, no, no!* You gotta make sure you're paying for that insurance and it remains valid, AJ. Thankfully on that deal I was able to get about $12,000 from the flood because I did that. You've got to make sure it's insured in both your business name (or whatever name that you're going to be holding it under) and the current owner/prior owner's name.

"There's definitely an element to all of this stuff that is a bit of a game. And it's important you know how to play it. So let's keep going. Next up in our list of OPM options: investors. With the right opportunity, it's actually relatively easy to line up private investors to give you money for the portion of the purchase price the bank needs you to pay. You'll need to put together a solid investment prospectus that outlines the potential return on investment (ROI) for the investors, but—in a perfect world you'd have already done that for the bank, so you should already have one ready to go."

"How're you doing, kid?" he said, enjoying watching AJ soak up every little last bit of what he said like a sponge. "Getting writer's cramp yet? You need a break?"

"Nah, I'm fine," said AJ, while humoring the old man by pretending to shake out his hand for effect and immediately assuming writing position once again. *I'm not sure how much of this I'm actually understanding at this point, but at least I'll have solid notes to refer back to when the time comes,* he thought to himself.

"OK, then—moving on. The next possibility would be Government Tax Credits. If you're looking at investing in properties that the government subsidizes—like affordable housing, for example—there are a bunch of different funding options such as a Rehabilitation Credit, Low-Income Housing Credit, and different tax credits for retrofitting properties with environmentally-friendly enhancements or rehabilitating certified historic structures, properties in disaster areas, etc. It's doubtful you'd want to enter any of these arenas straight out of the gate until you have at least a couple of deals under your belt, but it's good to know they exist, in case you stumble upon a property where it could be an option in future. They can be lucrative opportunities, but you need specialized knowledge in order to pull them off successfully. Let's just leave it at that for now, and you can research in more detail later if ever the need or desire arises.

"Last but not least is option six, cash flow from operations. I love the leverage of this one," Harold said, looking excited. "Imagine you come across an underperforming apartment building, for example, where the current landlord is renting the units at well below market rates. If you 'turned' those units, by putting in new tenants and raising the rent, you could increase your income dramatically. Another way you could do this would be to outfit each unit in the building with washers and dryers, or to do a cosmetic facelift, which could give you the ability to increase the rent by $25 to $50 per month per unit. Multiply that by hundreds of units, and that's a healthy increase in NOI."

"Hang on," said AJ, writing furiously. "That's a term I haven't heard before. You've talked about ROI, but what's NOI?"

"Net Operating Income, or NOI, is your income after expenses. It's important because banks value properties on NOI, not on market value. Therefore an increase in income can become an increase in value, which you can use to refinance by pulling money out of the property tax-free, and then putting that money into another real estate investment. Doing this over and over can significantly grow your portfolio—not to mention your wealth. Remember it this way: 'Any time you have an opportunity to increase NOI, you've got an opportunity for healthy ROI,'" Harold said with a smile.

"Now that your brain is full of acronyms like OPM, FHA, ROI and NOI, it's time to get down to the brass tacks. There are three basic expense types you'll need to pay attention to and account for: materials, labor, and permit costs. Regardless of what type of money you secure, you'll want to make sure you have double the amount of money to cover both the repairs (the combination of those three expense categories) and the amount of time you'll be paying the loan payments while the property is unoccupied."

"What do you mean?" AJ stopped writing and looked up at Harold with a furrowed brow. "Double the amount? Isn't that excessive?"

"If you're thinking, 'It's going to take me six months to complete a repair,' I want you to have at least *twelve* months of mortgage payments and the cost of the repairs put away at the highest payment price point. These things rarely, if ever, go as planned both time and money-wise. Better safe than sorry.

"And even though we've been talking about other people's *money* today, there are some additional 'other people' I want you to research and think about before our next meeting—your Power Team. They're another way to create leverage in your real estate investing business."

"Ooooh. Even though I have no idea what you're talking about, I certainly like the sound of it! What's a Power Team?" AJ's curiosity was piqued.

"Think of it as your rockstar speed dial list of everyone you're going to need to know to run a killer rehabbing business. Let's brainstorm a few to get you started," Harold said as he brought forth a clean page and his signature black marker. Together they bantered ideas back and forth until they had a pretty comprehensive list:

- Real estate professionals
- Mortgage broker(s)
- Real estate attorney/lawyer

- Accountant/Bookkeeper
- Tax professional
- Title company
- Appraiser
- Insurance agent/broker
- Contractor(s)/Handyman; Electrician, Plumber
- Bird dogs
- Bankers/Lenders
- Home inspector
- Termite folks
- Plumbing/HVAC
- Mentor/Coach
- Property manager
- Government Grant & Loan Specialist
- Surveyor
- Other investors

"Now that we've got the beginning of a list started for you, I want you to go back into research mode. First, look online and search 'Real Estate Investment Power Team' and go through other people's lists of the types of people you'll want and need on your team until you feel confident you haven't missed any major categories. Then start researching meetup groups for Rehabbing and Real Estate Investors in the area. Pretty soon you're going to need to leave the coffee shop and start interfacing with other people besides just me," Harold said, smiling. "And don't forget to have fun with it. You're on your way, kid."

"Will do!" AJ replied, grabbing his messenger bag and nearly knocking the table over as he jumped up from his seat. This was it—where the rubber hits the road. *Finally!* It seemed like things were really happening, and he was excited to get started. This was an area he knew nothing about, but he somehow felt like it was really important. *Maybe it's part of that gut feeling Harold was talking about?* he wondered to himself. *I think my intuition is starting to kick in.*

As AJ made his way to the café door, he heard a voice call to him from the register. Glancing over, AJ realized it was the friendly barista from earlier. He approached her with a smile.

"I'm sorry," he began, "I was deep in thought, and didn't catch what you said."

"Oh, I just wanted to properly introduce myself and give you this before you left," she said as she handed AJ a folded piece of receipt paper. "I'm Karen."

"Karen, it's nice to meet you." The two shook hands, Karen smiled, and then she disappeared into a back prep room. AJ unfolded the paper and discovered only ten digits scrawled across it—a phone number.

Reflexively, AJ looked in Harold's direction. Harold smiled knowingly and called out, "Positive momentum begets positive momentum."

ACTION ITEMS:

1. Put together a solid investment prospectus that outlines the potential ROI (return on investment) of a property. This can be used for the bank or potential investors. Include things like the neighborhood details, market value, funds required, the opportunities for the property and the cost of planned repairs, and outline the deal structure so an investor can properly assess it.

2. Develop your own "Power Team" list, including roles and potential people who might be a fit for any of the roles. Attend local meetups to connect with people involved in real estate investing, and ask if they have any referrals for great Power Team players. Meet with any potential Power Team members to see if you share values that are aligned and have good working chemistry, and ask them for any recommendations to fill the empty slots on your list, as well.

BEST PRACTICE:

Never go into a property rehab without double the amount of money you think you'll need to cover both the repairs and the loan payments while the property is going to be unoccupied.

CHAPTER NINE
KNOW YOUR NUMBERS

Don't ever let your business get ahead of the financial
side of your business. Accounting, accounting,
accounting. Know your numbers.
Tilman J. Fertitta

At their next meeting, Harold recapped his thoughts on finances for AJ.

"I mentioned before that your gut feelings develop over time. But as we've discussed, before the gut can kick in, you need to know your numbers. It's time to create a snapshot of your finances and get to know your numbers like the back of your hand.

"Today I'm going to give you your homework before the lesson even begins—in the same way I've been known to sometimes eat dessert before lunch," Harold said with a grin, motioning to the decadent pastry sitting in front of him. "The next assignment is to calculate your monthly expenses and how much you'll need to have saved to buy your first property, have enough for mortgage payments and fixes, and still keep your personal life on track.

"And in order for you to know what you'll need to do to keep your personal life afloat, you'll need to do a Personal Financial Statement."

"A what?" said AJ.

"A Personal Financial Statement, or PFS," Harold said, looking and sounding very official, "is a document or spreadsheet outlining an individual's financial position and cash flow at a particular point in time. It breaks down your income (what you make), assets (what you own), and your liabilities (what you owe). It's a document you'll need to prepare if and when you want to apply for a business loan, and it's a powerful tool to use on a regular basis to know your current position as it relates to money—tracking your goals and wealth, and understanding your overall financial health. There's no better time than the present to prepare your first one and start the process. Just like anything else, you need to practice knowing your numbers."

"Do you have a PFS document you can send me?" AJ asked, feeling a little intimidated.

"They're a dime a dozen," said Harold. "If you go online and search 'Personal Financial Statement,' there will be hundreds of templates that pop up. Take a look at a few different ones, so you can see both the similarities and differences between them. Then choose the one that feels right, and start to fill it out. You'll notice some have income and expenses on them, to show a bigger picture of your overall financial health, whereas others only show assets and liabilities and keep the income and expenses on a separate sheet called an Income Statement. Whichever one you choose, and whichever way you do it, make sure you're tracking all four components—assets, liabilities, income and expenses."

"OK, got it," AJ said, jotting down all four.

"And you'll need to keep it up to date with your finances as your business grows—this isn't a one-off thing," Harold warned. "Keep track of your business expenses and the ebb and flow of your finances. Money could be flying out the window and you won't realize it if you aren't looking at the numbers every week at a minimum—or even better, every day. Once you have a baseline and you know your starting point, start tracking right off the bat. It's one of the single most important keys to success in business."

"Definitely noted," AJ replied as he wrote.

"Continuing on with the idea of monitoring your numbers regularly, let's get back to that sore spot from our last meeting—your credit score. You need to be tracking your credit score monthly, just like you track the rest of your finances. You want to understand the fluctuations in your score, and what goes into the score you have. Roughly speaking, here's the information that is considered, and in what percentages," he said as he pulled out his marker and began scrawling notes on a page:

Payment History (35%)

Amount Owed (30%)

Length of Credit (15%)

New Credit (10%)

Types of Credit (10%)

"So how do I actually check my credit score?" AJ asked, feeling embarrassed.

"Start with something like CreditKarma.com. It's free, and you can check your credit as often as you want and continue to monitor it without it affecting your score. I like this program a lot, because the 'Insights' dashboard helps you learn what affects your credit score and helps you figure out what you can do to improve it on an ongoing basis. It's user friendly and explains things thoroughly—in terms you can actually understand when you're just getting started.

"There are creative ways to use credit to help and support your cash flow, but it's imperative that you take to heart the importance of using credit *responsibly*, AJ. In this day and age, it's incredibly sad because I recently read that millennials have racked up over US $1 trillion of debt. This amount has increased by more than 22 percent in just five years, and is more than any other generation in history! It's obvious to me that most of these people have never been taught how to use credit properly as a tool and a resource, and many of them are instead using it as a license to live beyond their means and use credit for retail spending. Once you're in the debt cycle, it's so unbelievably difficult to dig yourself out and make forward progress because when you get behind, you can't get ahead.

"But if used responsibly, credit is an important and powerful tool. There are some important tricks I can teach you; one, for example, is to utilize the paper checks that come in the mail as promotional offers that are tied to your credit card."

"I've never understood what those were for, so I've just always thrown them away thinking they were junk mail. Shoot. I should have saved them," AJ cringed.

"No worries. As long as your credit is good, they'll keep coming. And there's a deadline or 'use by' date, so any you might have saved would already be expired by now anyways. Not every card sends them, but Bank of America, Citi, and Discover cards are a few who often do. They're like a balance transfer option. This means that if you're carrying a balance on another card that is bearing interest, you can 'transfer' that balance to this card and get a 0% annual percentage rate (APR) for a specific number of months—but you'll usually have to pay a small fee for the privilege of doing this. The 0% interest period is for a fixed period of time, so if you exercise this option you'll want to make sure that you take the balance amount you've transferred, divide it by the number of months before the interest starts kicking in, and start making that monthly payment toward the balance so it's fully paid off before the interest would begin. For many of these checks, you can also write them to yourself to deposit and use for non-credit card balance transfers or to amortize purchases when you're being asked to pay the full amount up front."

"What do you mean by 'amortize purchases when you're being asked to pay the full amount up front?'" AJ asked.

"Well, there are certain companies who don't allow monthly payments for your purchase. For example, I just had to pay my annual membership dues of $5,000 for an important organization I belong to. Rather than burn my cash flow or pay interest by using a credit card normally, you could put it on a credit card that gives you points or cash back for your purchases (to get the cardmember benefit), and then use a promotional check with 0% interest to pay off that amount with a balance transfer. To amortize the purchase, you'd then set up an automatic payment for $416.67 per month to pay off the transferred amount (the total of $5,000 plus the balance transfer fee, divided by twelve) so that by the time the year was up you'd be paid off in full without having to outlay $5,000 all at once."

"Ahhh. I see," said AJ—the light turning on for him. "And in the rehabbing game, that strategy might also come in handy when I'm trying to finance short-term renovations and repairs for a property I'm going to fix and flip, right? I could get a balance transfer advance, pay for the repairs, and then sell the property and pay off the advance, right?"

"Exactly. Just remember to be diligent—and disciplined. And you'll need to allow enough time for the property to sell so you can pay it off before the full balance comes due and the advance starts bearing interest. You don't want to get caught with your proverbial pants down on this type of loan, AJ—if you miss the deadline, it's going to be a very expensive form of capital."

"Roger that," said AJ, his confidence growing.

"And as you continue to monitor your credit score, you'll look for new and creative ways to improve it. You'll want to keep tabs on the limits of your cards and steadily request limit increases—one at a time, slowly—and do whatever you can to keep the numbers looking strong and in your favor.

"There are plenty of other things you can do proactively to create a better cash flow position, too, beyond just reactively monitoring your numbers."

"Such as…? Can you give me an example?" AJ asked, eager to keep going.

"Sure, an example is when negotiating with vendors and partners. One important relationship on your Power Team will be with the contractor(s) you hire if you're going to be focused on rehabbing. So to create better cash flow when hiring contractors, clearly spell out a payment schedule that works for you and your cash flow, rather than just accepting whatever the contractor suggests. It'll vary depending on the size of the job and the region, but typically they'll ask for a one-third deposit with the balance upon completion. If you aren't planning to rent the property, consider offering them fifty percent up front and fifty percent when the property sells. NEVER, EVER make the final payment to your contractor until the job is *100%*

complete—including all small changes and issues you find during the final walkthrough. If you pay them before getting those final, niggly little details fixed, they'll rarely (if ever) get done—or it'll be six months and you needing to become a bit of a jerk before it happens."

"Ugh. That doesn't sound great. Maybe I'd be better off just doing it myself?" AJ wondered aloud.

"I would highly encourage you *not* to do that, AJ," Harold said firmly. "You really need to know your limits and stay within your zone of genius. That's one of my mantras for both rehabbing and life: 'Do what you can do well. And what you can't do well, hire well.'"

––––––––––––

Harold and AJ had started meeting in the mornings so that AJ would have the rest of the day to handle tasks that could only be completed during normal business hours. Today was slightly different, however—AJ had taken care of everything first thing in the morning, and he felt like he was actually beginning to get the hang of things himself.

Harold was drinking his afternoon green tea, but instead of sipping on anything himself, AJ nervously placed his Personal Financial Statement on the table. The other side of his paper included information about his chosen property and the loans he qualified for to make the property purchase a reality. It was one in Utah. Since Harold was so knowledgeable about Salt

Lake City and AJ had always wanted to own something near Downtown Salt Lake, he figured it was a good place to start.

"As I mentioned a few meetings ago, the first step is to open two business bank accounts. One checking and one savings."

"I actually did that after leaving here the same day you told me about it," AJ said, trying not to look as proud as he felt.

"Awesome—you're onto it!" Harold praised, feeling happy that his student was actually following through on his teachings.

"Step two is to save $250 to $500 a month, to be put aside for your cash flow business. That may be difficult in the beginning when you don't have a lot of income coming in, so you'll need to be mindful of your expenses. In fact, you'll want to be downright cheap at first. There's nothing wrong with starting a business on a shoestring budget—it's wise and prudent to be very methodical. Use an accounting software to track everything—there are some great low-cost, and even free, cloud-based options. This will allow you to easily monitor your numbers, reconcile your bank account transactions, track your expenses, and handle your taxes when the time comes."

"OK, got it. Should I put the money I'm saving every month into the same savings account I opened, co-mingled with the other stuff like the slush fund and security deposits?" he asked.

"Sure," Harold chuckled, "especially right now when I'm sure the only thing in there is the ten bucks or whatever was needed to actually start the account, right?"

AJ laughed. He may have felt slightly offended at this comment a few short weeks ago, but today he found it funny and nodded in agreement, feeling confident in his role as a budding entrepreneur and excited about being a student in a new game. He didn't care that he was starting at the bottom with next to nothing. At least he was getting started. *Huh*, he thought to himself. *My mindset is really changing right before my very own eyes. This practice and taking action stuff really works.*

Almost as if he read his mind, Harold went on to say, "Opening bank accounts and starting to save is all well and good. But that's not REALLY the most important action step in the process. Step three is the big kahuna—actually going out to *buy* that first rental property."

Oyyyyy. AJ's stomach did a little flip flop. It was hard to tell if this was fear, intuition, excitement, or what. He swallowed hard. "Do you think this is a good budget I've prepared and loan I've found? Am I ready to take the leap?" AJ realized everything suddenly felt very real and it dawned on him just how fast they had been moving through this. A moment of fear and hesitation gripped him like a vice.

"You're never going to cultivate a gut feeling just *talking* about getting into the game, and these big dreams of yours will never happen unless you jump in and take action," Harold said matter-of-factly. "There are three main steps to working the plan. Number one is finding and negotiating on the property, number two is the property inspection(s), and number three is planning and timelines. Since you're choosing the Utah property, I'll definitely be an asset. What's the worst that could happen? You might fall flat on your face, lose some money, and learn a lot. I say, go for it, AJ. It's all part of business. Welcome to the big leagues. And buckle up—this is the part where the ride may get a little bumpy," he said with a smile.

When AJ left that day, he knew it was the start of something promising and exciting—in a slightly nerve-wracking sort of way. He was meeting Karen that evening for dinner, after which he'd get a good sleep and spend the next morning doing exactly what Harold had advised—he was going to take the leap.

ACTION ITEMS:

1. Research options for accounting software (especially free ones when you're just starting), and set up an account so you can begin immediately tracking your cash flow and expenses.

2. Create your own Personal Financial Statement.

3. Open a free account with CreditKarma.com or another reputable company to check your credit score quarterly (set a reminder in your calendar for every three months to ensure you won't forget, and you can log your score each time in a running list in the notes section on your phone).

4. Calculate your monthly expenses and how much you will need to have saved to buy your first property. Be sure to factor in the mortgage payment and repairs for the rental property as well as your own personal monthly expenses.

5. Research credit cards with great benefits like frequent flyer points or cash back options, as well as those with regularly-recurring promotional balance transfer options (from two different banks).

BEST PRACTICE:
Get in the habit of looking at the numbers every week—or even better, every day. Keeping your finger on the pulse of your business will allow you to make informed financial decisions and will prevent you from unknowingly overspending on a project.

———————

BONUS BEST PRACTICE:
When hiring contractors, hire only licensed professionals to do your rehabs. Agreements should stipulate that any and all changes must be in writing and signed by both parties. Make sure they have an active certificate of insurance that includes property damage, general liability, workers compensation, and at least a $1 million umbrella policy they can add you/your company to as an additional insured party.

CHAPTER TEN
BUILD A SOLID FOUNDATION

You can't build a great building on a weak foundation.
You must have a solid foundation if you're going to
have a strong superstructure.
Gordon B. Hinckley

After making his first monthly deposit into his new savings account, AJ was feeling confident and ready to start getting organized in order to get his new business off the ground.

Looking around his apartment, he realized since getting fired he had never really taken the time to set up a proper workspace at home. The simple desk in the corner had been sitting—unoccupied—for months, and as he cracked open his laptop he felt a surge of excitement to start really getting serious about his new career path.

A quick Google search looking for "setting up a real estate investment business home office" yielded a ready-to-go checklist with everything he needed to get started.

It read:

What you'll need:

- Desk and chair
- Computer
- Real estate software; forms & contracts
- Phone (with voicemail)
- Professional email address
- Area map
- Camera (smartphone camera is fine, DSLR even better)
- Two-drawer file cabinet for legal size documents
- General office supplies

A desk and chair—check. Computer—check. Phone and voicemail—check. Camera—check. General office supplies—check. Not bad, he thought. *Only a few things I need to get.*

Fortunately the sparsely-decorated walls and lack of art in his apartment created a blank canvas for the large area map and whiteboard he just added to his online order. With a couple of extra clicks he secured a two-drawer file cabinet, some legal size manila folders and a label maker. He made a note to ask Harold about the software, forms and contracts at their next meeting, but as far as he could tell it seemed as though he was as ready as he felt he'd ever be.

He'd researched players for his Power Team, found a few meetups that looked interesting and added them to his calendar, and he was feeling good about the future. He was ready for his next meeting with Harold.

———————

"There's a common saying in real estate investing," Harold began—looking AJ square in the eye, with a serious look on his face. "People often say, 'You make your money when you buy.' Have you heard that before?"

"Yes—in fact I think you may have even said that to me a few times," AJ admitted, and then sheepishly added, "But truth be told, I don't actually know what you mean. Can you explain?"

"You make your money when you buy, not when you sell," Harold began. "This means that your purchase price is the main factor that determines your profit later on. You can't rely on appreciation, lower-than-projected construction costs, or wishful thinking to create your profit margin on the deal.

"And while we're on the topic of appreciation, let's do a deeper dive." Harold's eyes seemed to almost sparkle every time he spoke about financial gain. "With buy and hold properties, they will typically 'naturally' appreciate—or increase their value over time due to the increase in demand for the land. Because the world's population is constantly increasing, more people are looking for homes, and more properties are being built, so land becomes more and more expensive.

"With fix and flip properties, however, there's something called 'forced appreciation'. This refers to an increase in the value of a real estate investment property due to the investor's actions. Things you can do to 'force' appreciation include making cosmetic improvements (not major repairs), doing cleanups and minor repairs, pressure washing, painting, landscaping, replacing carpet/flooring, and increasing curb appeal."

"How do you determine which things to spend money on, and what to just leave alone?" AJ asked, his pen poised and ready to continue writing notes.

"I learned a bunch of that the hard way—through the school of hard knocks. The first property I bought, I fixed it up as if my wife and I were moving in. That seemed like logical reasoning to me at the time—do what needed to be done to create a home I would want to live in. We put blinds in. *Now I know*, however—you never put blinds in a fix and flip. There are certain rules for a fix and flip versus a place you would move into, or that you are fixing to rent. I've had to learn what those rules are. For example, while you never put blinds in a fix and flip—if it's for a rental, you *have* to do blinds. Most of the blinds I do now I get from Amazon—the two inch plastic blinds. I've learned over time the metal ones break so easily, so for just a little bit more, you can get some better ones off of Amazon. On a rental you can clean the carpets and if anything is wrong you can decrease the rent a little bit more. But carpet becomes a problem over time, and when it needs to be replaced you want to think about the long-term value. The main traffic areas wear out quickly, so I now replace them all with ceramic tile that looks like hardwood floor. I keep the carpet in the bedrooms, but in the main traffic areas I remove it. Think of it like this: you want to make minimal repairs to save on cost, but you still need to attract renters—and more renters means you can command higher rents and therefore increase your returns. You do this by making strategic repairs that balance your profitability with your renter's livability.

"Another example is to just do touch-up paint rather than painting the entire house if it's a rental. Right there, that could be a $10,000 savings. But if you're doing a fix and flip, you have to paint, and you have to get new flooring. And stainless steel appliances. I redo the countertops most of the time, and I've been putting a lot of granite in. With a rental, the appliances can be mismatched, but it needs to have a microwave, stove, and fridge. As I need to replace them one by one (when one breaks, for example), I replace it with one that's all black or stainless steel. I never do white anymore. If it's a less expensive home, I'll choose black appliances but if it's a higher-end home, I'll buy stainless steel and will ensure that the fridge, microwave and dishwasher match. I try to buy new appliances right around Thanksgiving, because I can get them cheaper during Black Friday sales. That's the lowest price. There are also little financing tricks you can use if you can't wait until that time of year, like buying from a retailer such as Best Buy, or a furniture company with an in-house credit card or credit terms, that offers some great financing options for 0% interest over a period of up to 72 months in some cases. Just like I explained earlier, this is a way of amortizing the new appliances and—if you're doing a fix and flip—you'll often be able to save cash flow and buy them on this 0% interest credit and then pay off the entire bill when you sell the property, never having paid a cent toward the new appliances until after the sale. This way you're maximizing your use of other people's money. Another way to manage your cash flow if you're not planning to rent the property and are doing a fix and flip is to consider offering your contractor 50% up front and 50% when the property sells.

"When you're doing a rental, remember it's all about the bedroom count and getting the highest rent value. When it's a fix and flip, you're making cosmetic changes (we call this 'putting lipstick on a property') and looking for the "wow" factor—like granite countertops.

Oh, man, AJ thought, feeling a little overwhelmed. *How am I ever going to get all of this stuff straight? These rules are more complicated than I thought they would be.*

As if reading his mind, Harold offered an encouraging smile. "Don't forget, kid—you're getting advice from someone who's been at it a long time and who has learned these rules over the course of *many* years. I'm just giving you the tips and tricks and hacks from my own experience and once you're up and running with a live test project this will all make more sense. Your own experience will be a great teacher, and my tips will just save you from making a bunch of mistakes I've already made... you're going to make your own mistakes—it's all part of the process. You don't have to worry about getting it perfect or completely 'right'. We're just making sure you've got enough information to be dangerous and give you a bit of a head start on the lessons."

"Thanks, Harold. I really *do* want to get it right, though. So let's keep going."

"All right. Let's talk about some other rehabbing tips and tricks I've learned over the years. While you go and grab another hot chocolate, I'll start making a list."

When AJ returned, Harold was hard at work penning his wisdom on a blank white page in his signature felt marker script. He didn't look up, and just started reading aloud.

Rehabbing tips & tricks:

- Key areas important to buyers are the kitchen, master bedroom, and bathrooms.

- Fixes that cost the least but provide the most value are flooring, painting, and landscaping.

- Try to use one—or no more than two—paint colors in all of your properties, and the same finish for each. We use Sherwin-Williams Repose Gray and Accessible Beige. Before you buy paint, check to see if the old paint is oil or latex (remember the rule oil over latex, but never latex over oil—it'll peel) and the finish (eggshell or satin) to make sure you're buying the right kind of paint. Bathrooms and kitchens often have oil paint as it is more resistant to moisture and water marks so be sure to check each room individually. Use

155

top-of-the-line self-priming paint (if you must use primer, consider tinting the primer the same color as the paint for easier coverage).

- Look into purchasing "scratch and dent" appliances for a discount or consider buying floor models.

- Dye carpet if possible (darker color carpets in bedrooms).

- Replace discolored or cracked electrical outlet plates.

- Upgrade cabinet and drawer handles by either getting new knobs and pulls or using the right spray paint to change the color.

- If cabinets are in bad shape, consider a new coat of paint.

- For countertop burns, make custom hot pads out of tile and save hundreds of dollars by not having to replace the whole counter.

- Paint/replace trim or add trim in places without it.

- Look for ways to improve the "curb appeal" of the home (new address numbers, lighting, little landscaping details, a nice mailbox)—small touches can go a long way, and the details do make a difference. Consider putting in a new front door if it needs it.

- Look for recycled or gently used fixtures and materials. Habitat for Humanity operates over

400 ReStore locations across the USA, which offer salvaged materials for low prices.

- Find the source of odors and remove them (pet odors, mold, hidden leaks, cigarette smoke, chemicals, blocked chimney, etc.). The fastest ways to remove odors caused by airborne particles are to change the filters, replace carpets if it makes sense financially and/or drapes, and use a paint that contains a primer-sealer.

- Other areas and items to address:
    - Roof
    - Chimney
    - Gutters
    - Windows
    - Doors & Locks
    - Decks & Porches
    - Heating/Furnace & A/C
    - Plumbing
    - Electrical
    - Floors
    - Walls
    - Bathrooms
    - Kitchen
    - Fireplaces
    - Skylights

- Foundation
- Basement
- Attic
- Leaks
- Ceiling repairs
- Kitchen appliances
- Driveway
- Dry rot
- Drywall repairs
- Odor issues
- Yard cleanup
- Light fixtures
- Closet organizers

Wow, thought AJ, there's so much to learn! This only excited him more, and he couldn't wait to get his first project on the go.

"So what are the actual steps I'll need to go through in the process to actually buy a property?" AJ asked, feeling impatient. He imagined himself as a racehorse behind the starting gate, antsy to get going; he was itching to run free—and fast.

"There are eight main steps, split into two parts. In part one, you'll locate and identify potential properties, evaluate them by putting together the numbers and analyzing the transaction, and then you'll negotiate the agreement and have the contract prepared and signed. In part two, you'll open escrow, satisfy all contingencies, assign the contract or close the transaction, and then either fix up and rent (buy & hold) or fix up and sell (fix & flip). This is just a broad overview, but that's the gist of the process you'll follow for each transaction from start to finish.

"There are a lot of tasks inside each step—far too many to go through here—but there are a few pearls of wisdom and nuggets of advice I've learned that will be helpful. For example, when locating and identifying potential properties, remember the golden rule: don't buy the nicest or most expensive product… aim rather to buy the worst house on the best street. Do property inspections. Pull permits (structural, electrical, roof, plumbing, and windows)—not pulling them can result in wasted time, labor and money. Hire only licensed professionals to do your rehabs. Do all the demolition inside first. Landscape early to attract attention. When you're ready to sell, start selling it while you're doing the inside. Offer a 'referral fee' to the neighbors. And get the buyer pre approved."

"I have a feeling these tips and tricks are going to save me a LOT of money and heartache, Harold. Thank you. I am truly grateful for your help. I've been narrowing down my list of potential properties and evaluating the numbers, and after this session with you today I'm pretty sure I know which one is my top choice and I'm going to go ahead and make an offer on it. Thinking ahead, and dreaming big, I have one last question: after I close my first deal and the cash is in the bank after the flip, what do I do with that money? Do I just put a hundred percent of it back into the next deal?"

"That would be the dream," Harold said with a smile, looking starry-eyed, "But no. The money from the deal needs to be split up. Part of it is saved for the next deal, part is pooled for personal finances, and part is for a partner's share—if you eventually decide to get a partner, of course."

AJ confidently put his notes into his bag and stood up. "Wish me luck!" he called over his shoulder to Harold as he walked toward the door.

"Luck is the marriage of when preparation meets opportunity. And you're ready—it's time—you don't need my wishes. Go get 'em, kid."

AJ smiled to himself as he reached the door. Giving a quick glance over at the counter before walking out, he saw Karen looking at him. She mouthed the words, "Good Luck," and gave him a thumbs up sign.

Here goes nothing, he thought, walking out of the café and into his future.

ACTION ITEMS:

1. Setup your workspace so you have the tools you need to get your business underway.

2. Talk to your mentor about his or her top Fix & Flip vs. Buy & Hold "Rules." Each investor will have learned different lessons throughout their career which will influence the tips and tricks they feel are most important. This is also a great conversation topic at real estate investor meetups when you hit an awkward silence when speaking with new people you meet.

3. Find your local Habitat for Humanity ReStore (or other secondhand building supply shop) and start to visit every few weeks so you know what type of materials you can source from there.

4. Start a spreadsheet to budget your rehab costs - there are some great templates you can find to start with just by doing a quick internet search.

BEST PRACTICE:

Get a licensed home inspection. The cost is typically somewhere around $350, depending on the size of the property. It will save you from surprises and give you the start of an action plan for rehabbing the property.

CHAPTER ELEVEN
DO YOUR HOMEWORK

Nothing is more powerful for your future than being a
gatherer of good ideas and information. That's called
doing your homework.
Jim Rohn

Now that AJ had completed his first fix and flip, he'd begun
researching new real estate markets. After reading a lot of articles
about the latest trends in the industry, he discovered business
was moving toward the center of the country.

His first deal in Utah had been a success, large in part due to the
sound advice Harold had given him. There were definitely some
hiccups along the way, but because he had taken the proper
steps and had enough of a buffer in his slush fund account, he'd
been able to tackle everything that popped up. And because he
knew to expect some issues, he didn't let it bother him much
and considered it part of the process. That first door also gave

him the cash flow to acquire more rental properties. Where should he buy next?

Two houses in Tulsa, Oklahoma had recently caught his eye. They were $66,000 apiece and would bring in about $700 a month in rent. Each one seemed like a great investment to AJ, but he wasn't totally certain because his knowledge of the Oklahoma market was nothing more than what his cursory readings online had been able to provide. Unsure, AJ found Harold's number—still in his 'Favorites'—and hit send.

"Hey, AJ! So nice to hear from you. What's happening?"

AJ relayed the details of his property predicament and waited patiently as Harold considered all of the facts.

"They're overpriced, AJ," he began. "I can get units that bring in $650 a month in rent at $30,000 each. I think what you're looking at are actually duplexes at $66,000 a door."

AJ reeled from this fact—he was certain they had been two distinct houses with their own lots and property.

"I just bought a duplex for $25,000 a door going for $500 a month in rent," Harold continued. The duplexes you're looking at are about $650 to $750 a month for rent. But I wouldn't know all of this if I hadn't done my homework two months ago. I've been researching the area myself."

"So," AJ replied slowly, "I shouldn't invest here?"

"Well, I wouldn't say that. I wouldn't buy those particular properties at a total of around $129,000 with closing costs, but—if you're spending that much money anyway—why don't you buy a duplex for $160,000 that's in a much better area and in much better condition?"

Thinking about all of the headaches a property in poor condition would cause, especially at such a distance, AJ mentally conceded that spending the extra money now would pay off in the long run. Why hadn't he thought of that? *This is why Harold is the expert, after all.* The idea of a duplex was interesting—he hadn't thought of that before, either. One mortgage, but with two rental income opportunities. It mitigated the risk substantially if he had a tenant leave with a gap before he could get someone new in, because he'd still have the other tenant paying rent. *Hmmm. I like that idea a lot.*

"OK, AJ, I'm going to give you some homework." *Just like the old days*, AJ thought to himself. "But first, where did you get those original comparables?"

"Well..."

"Actually, it's not important. Part of your homework is to call other agents, not the same firm that gave you the comps you have."

After pulling out a memo pad, AJ started to jot down notes, careful to record everything Harold was saying and silently kicking himself for not pulling out the pad sooner.

"OK, I can do that. How many agents should I call?"

"Start with one. Ask what areas they recommend and what neighborhoods are best and so forth. Remember, you want this $800,000 to be spread over multiple properties—two, three, four different duplexes. See what the agent tells you and if you're getting conflicting information, get another opinion.

"But don't sign a buyer-broker agreement. Tell them you're just in an exploratory period." Harold stopped for a moment and AJ eagerly waited for him to continue. After a second more, he asked, "This money—that $800,000—do you need that money today?"

"Uh, no… not exactly," AJ stuttered, slightly surprised by the query.

"OK, great. This sounds like a retirement investment. That means this is sacred money and you have to treat it that way. There are real estate agents that will be more than happy to help you with these comps. Find them and take your time."

"But don't I have to move quickly since I'm doing a 1031 exchange to defer capital gains?" AJ knew the rules and didn't want to mess this up, but he also didn't want to disappoint Harold or not follow some sage advice.

"You don't want to rush into anything just to get that money deployed," Harold assured. "Do your research and make sure you're putting that money in the best place possible. Otherwise, we're going to be having this same conversation in a few months."

"But how do you know if something is the best deal?"

Harold chuckled. "Kid, remember: you don't get gut feelings until you've done your homework. I've done enough research and have seen how markets work long enough that I don't even need access to the MLS to know if something feels off with a deal. But you don't get there without putting in the work.

"Make sure you ask many, many questions: How long do tenants stay here for? Am I going to have to put a new A/C unit after each tenant because they're going to take it with them? Will you have to put in new appliances after someone moves out? Have you managed properties in this neighborhood before? Have you been to these properties? Are you willing to go there during the day or do you need to carry a gun with you?"

A giggle escaped AJ before he could stop it. The question seemed silly and a bit ridiculous—he couldn't *imagine* asking a firm or an agent something like that.

"You laugh," Harold commented, "but I know friends in other states who purchased properties for five, ten, twenty thousand dollars and are now trying to *give* away their properties because of this. If an agent's not willing to go there without a gun in the middle of the day, it's probably not something you want."

"You've really had friends trying to give away properties like that?" AJ couldn't believe it.

"Oh, yes. Cheap properties are not for the faint of heart. They can totally turn a beginner off. Nearly every time I've tried it, I've had to put new copper plumbing in or a new A/C and heater—it just wasn't worth it."

Isn't there SOME way to start with a cheaper property? AJ thought. *I had to take out a pretty hefty loan for my first property, and I want to get into something less expensive.* As if reading his mind, Harold had advice on a way around these problematic cheap properties.

"Cheap properties can be a challenge but a mobile home or a trailer may be an option for the low-budget investor. I'd rather have somebody get a mobile home to fix and flip or use it as a lease option than buy one of those really cheap things."

"But don't most mobile home parks have a rule against renting them out?"

"That's why you do seller financing," Harold explained. "I've done that before and doubled my money."

"Did you start with mobile homes or trailers when you first started investing and then work up from there?"

"I started with single family homes, because that's what I was most comfortable with. Plus, if you need to sell an asset, a single family home usually sells quicker even if you have to sell it for a loss. There are more end-user buyers than investor-buyers out there looking for homes to live in when a market is bad. But I still think about that darn trailer park—the one that got away. I guess you win some and you lose some," said Harold, sounding nostalgic.

"I guess what I was getting at before was, what signs do you look for to know something is a bad deal after you do your research? Or *while* you're doing it, rather?" asked AJ, feeling worried about getting into a bad deal.

"Having a checklist is good: Are there any homes in the neighborhood that are boarded up? Are there any other foreclosures? How are the other homes in the area? Take note of everything from the exterior of the property to the building and landscaping. But just because there's a boarded up home, an unkempt lawn, or a foreclosure doesn't mean it's a nasty area—you can't stop digging there. If it's something close by, I would go there and 'walk the house' myself.

"Some people can do it on numbers and research alone, but I've just never been that guy. From the very beginning of my investing career, I had to see it; I had to smell it. Doing that gave me not just a sense of the property, but also the neighborhood. And, depending on how often you feel the need to check-in on your buy and hold rentals, it might make more sense to manage them yourself—at least initially—instead of getting a property manager. But all of that comes a bit later."

"What if there are a lot of renters in the area?" AJ asked. "That's good, right? It means people want to live in that part of town."

"If it's mainly renters in the neighborhood, that obviously means there are mainly rentals. They're all going to be your competition. That being said, it isn't a no-go if it's mostly rentals. Just know when you are up for vacancy and advertise appropriately. I would definitely make sure to understand when most turnovers happen in that area."

"What do you mean? Like when people typically move out?"

"Yep," Harold confirmed. "For example, in Boston it's September first. According to *Real Estate Boston*, around eighty percent of the leases start September first—which makes sense because it's a college town. Also consider that people often move with the seasons. No one is thrilled to be making a move in the northern states in the middle of winter, so the demand for rentals is much higher in the warmer months. The easiest way to get somebody back into your unit is being aware of these cycles. Part of that is making sure your rentals become vacant during those time periods. You need to set your lease dates accordingly."

"OK," AJ was reasoning through this information. "Let's say you're able to walk the neighborhood, you've visited the area, but you still only have a basic knowledge of the market. How do you find out about these cycles?"

"You make friends," Harold shot back with a laugh. "You really need to talk to some property managers to figure it out because some areas are counterintuitive. For example, Florida is an exception to the winter issue I just mentioned. It rents best in the winter because all of the snowbirds come down to escape the cold."

"And… property managers will just tell you that information?"

"That's where a bit of legwork comes in. You're probably going to have to call five to eight of them to get two or three to call you back. Investors scare property managers off because they aren't a sure lead. But, honestly, we're getting ahead of ourselves. Start with the homework I gave you and we'll go from there."

"This might be getting ahead of myself, too, but I was also wondering about something I heard a guy mention the other day. He was talking about putting his properties into different LLCs. Do you do that?"

"Yes. I try to put about a million dollars' worth of properties per LLC—which for me is typically three or four properties. If it's a commercial property, I put it in its own LLC. I'm not an attorney, so let's be clear… I'm not giving you any legal advice here… this is just how I do things personally. And I have an umbrella insurance policy that's a $3 million umbrella policy, and each property has homeowners and renter's insurance on top of that."

I can't wait to have enough properties to have to think about this stuff! I'll at least start with the insurance part now, and look forward to the rest later.

After AJ and Harold exchanged farewells and hung up, AJ turned to his computer and pulled up a search of real estate agents in the Tulsa metro. He had work to do.

ACTION ITEMS:

1. Work with more than one real estate agent, especially when it's in a city you aren't familiar with. This lets you gather additional information and perspectives so you can learn more.

2. Research the neighborhoods you are looking at investing in. How well are properties taken care of? What are the rental patterns? If you can, go and walk or drive by the property.

3. Connect and build relationships with property managers in the areas where you have rental properties. They will have a wealth of knowledge and you may choose to use their services when your cash flow allows.

BEST PRACTICE:
Don't be fooled into thinking the cheaper the house, the better the return. Some houses are in undesirable areas and will be tough to flip regardless of how nice the rehab is.

CHAPTER TWELVE
GIVE BACK

There is no finish line. There are only mile markers.
Michael Ventura

It had been five years since AJ's initial meeting with Harold, and a lot had changed.

AJ's date with Karen from the café had progressed quickly into a serious relationship, and AJ had eventually proposed.

He and Karen now lived in a large house in Santa Monica; it wasn't quite the Malibu home from his vision board, but it was definitely one made better than the brick and mortar it was built from because he had Karen living there alongside him.

The only thing that hadn't changed much in five years was AJ's mentor-mentee relationship with Harold. He still consulted him before any new deal and weighed Harold's perspective against his own when making major financial decisions. But, as always, he did his homework first—just as he'd been taught.

Harold smiled when he saw AJ's name appear on his phone, and swiped to answer the call on the first ring. "What's up, kid?"

"I'm in town for a couple of days, and I'd love to see you and catch up," AJ said with a grin. "Meet you at the office tomorrow morning first thing?"

For the first time in their relationship, AJ beat Harold to the café and had a mug of black tea waiting on the table for him when he arrived. After a friendly catch up, the conversation naturally turned to investing.

"So, now that you've been in the game for a handful of years—what do you think of your career choice?" Harold asked AJ with a smile.

"Well—like anything—there are definitely ups and downs, but I do have to say I really enjoy the lifestyle, and I love working for myself. One thing's for sure: I could never have done it without you, Harold. Thank you so much for your advice and guidance over the years." Gratitude emanated from every ounce of AJ's being, and his words were filled with deep and authentic appreciation.

"Hey kid, it's my pleasure! I enjoy sharing my knowledge and helping others discover their path—especially when it includes real estate. Makes me feel like all my lessons over the years are worth even more when it's not just me learning from them," Harold chuckled. "And now... there's one final lesson I want to share with you. You're far enough into your journey, and I think you've gained enough experience; it's time for you to learn how to become an 'Old Timer,'" he said proudly, like a parent about to initiate a child through a special rite of passage in life.

"You mean like the secret little club of people you told me about who are doing all the deals in advance at Denny's before the auctions at the county steps? Geez. While I appreciate your confidence, I don't think I've made *anywhere near* the level of relationships I need for that kind of move yet, Harold." AJ looked visibly nervous.

"While that is certainly one of the strategies an Old Timer might employ, that's not the one I was meaning in this case," Harold said, laughing. "It's time for me to introduce you to the Mac daddy of the real estate investing world: portfolio income. Once you build up a portfolio of properties that are covering their own costs and becoming profitable, there are still other ways you can derive income from real estate. Do you remember the day when we were sitting here and you had that huge breakthrough—when you had the lightbulb moment about active and passive income streams? You may not remember, because we didn't go into any further detail at the time, but there are actually *three* types of income: earned—or active—income, passive income, and portfolio income.

"Portfolio income is when your money begins to make money for you—typically through interest," Harold explained.

There's always so much more to learn, thought AJ.

Harold continued, "Most portfolio income gets favorable tax treatment. Dividends and capital gains are taxed at a lower rate than earned income. In addition, portfolio income is not subject to Social Security or Medicare taxes. Some types of real estate-related portfolio income you'll be familiar with, like seller financing and hard money lending. But ones you might not know about yet are tax lien auction investments, discount note buying and venture capital."

AJ was still getting his head around all of the aspects of his current active and passive income streams and he wasn't so sure he was ready for these next steps. He decided to gently change the subject.

"Well, now that you mention the word 'portfolio,' I *have* recently picked up a couple mobile homes and trailers as low-cost fix and flips. I'm trying to balance my portfolio out a bit," AJ replied.

"Diversifying is a great way to make sure if a specific area or sector of the market has a downturn, your entire portfolio doesn't suffer."

"And because I had built relationships with a couple of real estate agents in the area when I was buying those properties, I recently caught wind of a distressed seller looking to offload their trailer park." As he spoke, AJ reached under his chair to pull out a black gift box with a luxurious red ribbon tied in a bow on top. He placed the box in front of Harold and said,

"I'd like you to have this. It's the least I can do after everything you've done to help me."

Harold looked touched as he opened the box to find a draft sale and purchase agreement for the trailer park, with his name listed as the purchaser. He looked up at AJ with surprise in his eyes. "Wow! I must have taught you well if you managed to negotiate this price!"

"I learned from the best. And I thought it might go a little way to soothe the pain from the 'one that got away' you mentioned years ago," AJ said, feeling proud of how much he had achieved in the last five years. That call center job felt like a lifetime ago.

AJ felt the need to continue. "A couple of years ago, a friend recommended an incredible book to me called *The Go-Giver,* which features a mentor and a protégé—just like us—and teaches how shifting your focus from being a 'Go-Getter' to becoming a 'Go-Giver' is the secret to stratospheric success. The entire time I was listening to it on audiobook, I just couldn't help but think about how you really embody the spirit of the values they were describing, Harold. You've always been a Go-Giver. And this is such a great opportunity for me to *finally* feel like I can give something meaningful back to you in return."

"AJ, it's been so great to mentor someone with the drive and dedication you have shown these past five years. And this gift means more to me than you'll ever know. Thank you for this deal; I think it's one of the most thoughtful gifts I've ever received." Harold's eyes shone in the light, revealing what looked like glassy tears that had formed as he spoke. His energy quickly changed, and a twinkle replaced the tears. "Ha! The one that got away. I'm comin' for you this time! I can't wait to drive by and check it out!" Harold exclaimed with an exuberant laugh.

"Me neither. And—I'm not gonna lie—I'm a *little bit* nervous that I might have missed something," AJ replied with a candid laugh.

"Well, shall we finish our drinks and head over there?" Harold said eagerly as he downed what was left of his tea.

"Let's go," said AJ with a smile, feeling pleased to have been able to do something for Harold in return for the years of wisdom and time he had shared. In a single moment, he finally understood the famous quote by Winston Churchill, "We make a living by what we get. We make a life by what we give."

The End

CONCLUSION

During the journey of writing this book, I was thrown into a whole new journey alongside it: fighting cancer. It all started with a small pain in my side, and then—not even two weeks later—I was having surgery where they found a tumor, which had pierced my appendix and caused it to burst. We got to the bottom of the stomach pain, but found a whole other challenge ahead.

It was so hard to break the news to our children. They just kept saying, "This isn't real." My wife, Andrea, was there for me from day one, encouraging me to see a doctor at the outset of the stomach pain and being there for surgery and everything that came after. It was a rough and long road going down. Just the day before, we had booked a trip to Hawaii with our neighbors—what were we going to do with that? There were so many unanswered questions. We had so many ups and downs. We needed answers, we needed peace, we needed a miracle. So, after much reflection, an email was sent out to the church to fast and pray for us, and I sent out individual texts to friends, neighbors, colleagues, and family to fast and pray for me. It was a humbling experience. One I am grateful for.

If you know me, you know I dive into things and learn all I can on a topic—and my health journey was no different. I poured myself into researching. I lined up calls. I scheduled appointments and tests. I researched. I decided to put myself on a raw vegan diet. I had heard and read that sugar and other unhealthy eating habits feed cancer, and this was one thing I could control and help fight against my cancer.

I went through chemo—both intravenous and in pill form—and lost a lot of weight. I've had a number of surgeries, and have tried a lot of different treatments. Cancer began to occupy my (and my wife's) every waking thought. I used to spend at least 80% of my day thinking about my business. The changes we were going to have to make to our lives after the diagnosis were hard to imagine. I had to accept that I was in survival mode and needed a caregiver, and that I didn't have the same energy for my relationships and the way my life used to be. I am a go-go-go kind of guy, and even the *thought* of slowing down was extremely tough for me, let alone the reality.

Throughout my journey, I am often asked, "Aaron, how can you have cancer and be so positive?" It's a good question, and my answer is: mindset. Andrea suggested I look at my health situation like a business (my business right now personally is to live, to stay alive, and overcome this disease that I have) and to look at this as an investment in my health. She knows how to push me.

I stepped back and asked myself what I had control over. I listed these things:

- What I eat

- The doctors I choose to see

- What I put into my body (chemo and other meds)

- Alternative treatments I choose to do

- What I take into my mind

And then I focused on taking control of each of these items I have control over.

I have three kids, and a wonderful wife who loves me—she is my ROCK. I have an AWESOME business, and amazing business partners I choose to work with all across the country. I have TOO MUCH to live for. I WANT to LIVE, I WANT to experience this life with my wife, family and kids. I know what my prognosis is but I don't share it with anyone. I don't care to know it, I don't want you to tell me, I don't want to talk about it. Instead I choose to talk about what I can do to be part of the 1-2% of people that beat the HELL out of this disease and survive. What did they do to BEAT THIS? I don't want to be normal, I don't want to be another statistic—good or bad. (And I am already not a statistic any longer since I'm no longer doing full-dose chemo.) What do I have to do to be that 1-2% of successes that just wipe this out of their system quickly?

I have had to research what others have done to heal themselves. I treat this like business, and that is my RAD (rip off and duplicate). I have been working this way for twenty years—I follow what others do, how they make their money, and now I'm applying that to my health. I started to talk to and research how people with the type of cancer I have *lived*. What they did, what they ate, the supplements they took and treatments they underwent. I am doing those things.

Because I know how hard this journey is, I want to share it with others. I am building up a list of my findings and sharing them on aaronmarshall.com/resources. If you have any questions, please contact me directly through my health journey blog site at https://aaronmarshall.com, as I want to be able to support anyone who is embarking on a similar journey. I've learned that it really helps to have a lot of support around you, which I am eternally grateful for, and I want to pay that forward.

Of course when you are diagnosed with appendix, colon and liver cancer you have some tough times. Funny enough, though, even though it was written before my diagnosis, one of the early themes of this book was mindset, and it holds just as true in battling cancer as it does in real estate investing (or anything else in life, for that matter). I've accepted this is my journey and my life, and my inspiration comes from others and from God. Even more so now, I encourage people to find their passion and follow it. Life is precious, and I hope this book has given you the tools and inspiration to begin building your own cash flow business so you can focus on what matters most: *living*.

RECOMMENDED READING

- *Rich Dad, Poor Dad* by Robert Kiyosaki

- *The 'Highest and Best' Real Estate Investment* by Mike Watson

- *Start with Why* and *Find Your Why* by Simon Sinek

- *The Total Money Makeover* by Dave Ramsey

ABOUT THE AUTHOR

Over the past 19 years, Aaron Marshall has bought and sold over 1,500 properties, including 'fix & flip', bank foreclosures, notes, the county courthouse steps, and long-term buy & hold investment properties.

Co-Founder & CEO of Keyrenter Franchise, a nationwide residential property management company, Aaron champions exceptional customer service, communication, and outstanding management of real estate assets. Ranked #1 property management company in their markets on Yelp and Google, Keyrenter Franchise also made <u>Entrepreneur's Annual Top 500</u> Franchise List and ranked 25 on the list of Top 100 New Companies, recognizing innovative services, marketing methods, and technologies.

Aaron continues to buy and sell real estate for himself and is always on the look out for Single-Family, Multi-Family, and Commercial real estate deals.